# FROM
# PRODIGAL
# TO
# PRIEST

# FROM PRODIGAL TO PRIEST

DAVID CHADWELL

20th Century Christian Foundation
2809 Granny White Pike
Nashville, Tennessee
37204

# Table of Contents

# Chapter One

# Convinced or Converted?

Casual observation will reveal that the American society is composed of distinctive groups: the "involved" group; the "amen" group; the "it is alright with us" group; and the "I could care less" group. The "involved" group finds it natural to champion causes actively. The "amen" group believes in and advocates causes, but it limits its support to being well-wishers. The "it is alright with us" group's involvement is limited to not being a hindrance. The "I could care less" group is apathetic with no concern.

These groups also exist in the Lord's church. Their existence in the church has produced two frightening situations. First, it has produced an alarming number of Christians with no sense of spiritual commitment. Their greatest act of commitment is to say, "Amen", or, "It is alright with us." Second, it has produced numbers of Christians who are spiritually incapable of coping with any crisis. Years of apathetic "okaying" have robbed them of all spiritual strength. The lives of the "amen" Christians, the "it is alright with us" Christians, and the "I could care less" Christians consist of little more than a few habits built around attending worship. It is frightening to see how many of them live in fear and depression.

How can the same Savior influence one Christian to become an involved, fulfilled person radiantly alive in Christ, and produce nothing but apathy in another Christian? How can any Christian know the Lord, understand the Word, taste the promises, be a part of the Lord's family, and still be weak or indifferent? Obviously, many problems create apathy and disinterest. However, a major contributor to the situation is this: too many Christians have been convinced but not converted.

## *The Convinced Person*

There is a vast difference between being convinced and being converted. Being a convinced person is not difficult. He believes God exists, Jesus is the Son of God, the Bible is divine truth, and all need to be saved. He is convinced that God should be obeyed, that Jesus is the true religious authority, and that one must be a member of the Lord's church and worship regularly. However, his faith is only a shallow, intellectual understanding.

*His believing and being convinced is no more than accepting a set of facts.* A convinced person regards his beliefs as important, but not as imperative. While strongly feeling one should do what is right, his doing right is not a matter of urgency. He has no devastating awareness of past sinfulness or of having been lost. Thus, he feels no sense of rescue from death or deliverance from destruction. Feeling has little place in his Christian life or his spiritual motivations. He may even object strongly to religious feelings. He has reduced the whole Christian life to a set of facts to be accepted.

Since faith and understanding is merely possessing proper facts, he accepts the facts, builds a few necessary new habits, and continues to live a "normal" life. His life is simple, easy, and involves no hard decisions. He is comfortable with his life and assures himself everything is fine because he has accepted the right facts. He enjoys the ultimate convenience of living without conscience problems.

## *The Converted Person*

In complete contrast, being converted is not simple or easy. Being converted hurts. This person looks honestly at hard realities about himself. He sees his own sins for what they are. Admitting he is responsible for his sins, he accepts accountability for his life. He acknowledges that just condemnation and punishment will result if his sins are not forgiven. All of that hurts.

*Being converted is a life-shattering experience.* Before conversion he was deceived in his belief that he controlled his life. He discovered sin controlled him. He understands what his sins are and how they have offended God. He confesses his life has not been good, right, or okay, and he admits it is his fault. These acknowledgements so tear his world apart he knows he *must* change.

*Being converted involves a moment of terrible fear and despair.* Realizing he is lost, he knows he is powerless to rescue himself from sin. From the depths of his heart, he knows he cannot save himself. In life's most terrifying moment, he sees and faces eternal destruction.

*Being converted demands repentance and resurrects the conscience.* Repentance involves many hard decisions. The conscience makes him a person who thinks rather than a person who reacts to circumstances. He now answers to himself and to God on a daily basis.

*Being converted is finding a Savior.* He allows Jesus to destroy the enslaving guilt, fear, and anxiety founded in his past life. He accepts the peace, direction, and hope promised in conversion. Conversion is demanding because it involves the whole person — mind and heart, knowledge and emotions, body and soul.

## *Examples of Conversion*

There are three excellent examples of the process and the results of being converted. *The Christians at Thessalonica are the first.* No more than a month after Paul and Silas established that congregation, they incurred the wrath of jealous Jews who hired the riffraff to start a riot (Acts 17:5). Some of the Christians were dragged before rulers of the city and forced to pay a peace bond. The brethren so feared for Paul and Silas that they sent them away by night.

After he left, Paul wrote I Thessalonians to those Christians. In chapter one he extols their work of faith, labor of love, and steadfastness of hope. Rather than discouraging them from imitating the faith and lives of Paul and Silas, the afflictions made them an example of faith, godliness, and commitment to Christians throughout Greece.

Considering their stormy beginning, one must ask, "How could such spiritual development occur under such circumstances?" How could they learn to be exceptional Christians with the limited opportunities of troubled conditions? 1 Thessalonians 1:9, 10 gives the answer:

> For they themselves report concerning us what manner of entering in we had unto you; and how ye turned unto God from idols, to serve a living and true God, and to wait for his Son from heaven, whom he raised from the dead, even Jesus, who delivered us from the wrath to come.

Why were they exceptional Christians? They deliberately gave up their past religious life to come to the living God. They came to the living God with the desire and commitment to serve. They were more than convinced. They were converted.

*The second example is the Christians in Rome.* In Romans 6 Paul reminds them of the basic realities of being in Christ. Baptism into His death placed them in Christ (v. 3). Resurrection from baptism's burial brought newness of life (v. 4). The body of sin had been deliberately crucified to end bondage to sin (vv. 6, 7). They were now dead to sin and alive to God (v. 11). Sin would not be allowed to reign in their bodies or to use their bodies (vv. 12–14). They belonged to the one they obeyed (v. 16).

Verses 17, 18 declare:

> But thanks be to God, that, whereas ye were servants of sin, ye became obedient from the heart to that form of teaching whereunto ye were delivered; and being made free from sin, ye became servants of righteousness.

Serving sin was a part of their former life. When they obeyed from the heart the pattern of teaching given them, they ceased being slaves to sin. Now they willfully were servants or slaves of righteousness. These people had been more than convinced; they were converted.

*The third example is the well-known prodigal son of Luke 15:11–32.* A man's youngest son demanded his inheritance and received it. Shortly thereafter he left home for a far country. There he wasted the entire inheritance in foolish, irresponsible living. A severe famine forced him to accept the disgraceful job of feeding a Gentile's hogs. His hunger was so great he gladly would have eaten the carob tree's husky pods with the hogs if they had been digestible. No one helped him; no one cared about his need; no one gave him anything.

Luke 15:17 says, "But when he came to himself . . ." *Conversion begins with coming to oneself.* In sin, no one sees, thinks, or understands clearly. In sin, no one is ever truly himself. When the prodigal came to himself, he realized his father could care for his needs. He knew he needed to return to his father and to confess his sin against his father and God. He clearly understood his unworthiness to be regarded as a son. Willingly confessing the truth, he would request his father make him a hired servant.

The result of "coming to himself" was this: he got out of the pigpen and started walking home. How difficult that trip must have been! What anxieties and fears must have haunted him as he drew nearer that fateful meeting with his father!

Through those long months the father never ceased watching for the return of his son. Though the son was likely ragged, dirty, and thin from hunger, the father recognized him in the distance. With compassion, joy, and thankfulness, he ran to meet his son. Hugging and kissing him, the father hardly let him utter his confession. After being clothed and receiving a family ring, the son was honored with a feast of thanksgiving and rejoicing. The son who was dead was now alive.

The turning point in this rebellious young man's life was coming to himself. Finally, in the pigpen he saw himself for what he was. He honestly realized what he had done. He clearly saw his mistakes and unworthiness. He knew he had to do something; he knew he had to redirect his life. Thus he got out of the pigpen, got on the road, and went home to throw himself on his father's mercy. That is the most beautiful, forceful example of conversion in the New Testament.

*If New Testament Christians are to exist, the nature of a converted person must be understood clearly.* There are three aspects of conversion. The first is recognition. The person in absolute honesty recognizes who he is, what he has done, and what his immediate condition is. The second is awareness. He is aware that it is imperative that his life change. Whatever the price, he *must* change. He cannot tolerate continuing as he is. The third is a "becoming." When the person he was before conversion is compared to the person he is after conversion, it is like seeing two different people. His actions, attitudes, purposes, desires, and feelings are different. He has become a new person in Christ.

## Why So Many Unconverted?

One troublesome question remains. Why are there so many unconverted persons in the church? First, the situation exists because of a failure in teaching. It is a failure produced by misunderstanding, not an intentional failure. *People have been allowed to substitute "belonging to the church" for being converted to Christ.* In the Scriptural sense those converted to Christ have been added to the church by God (Acts 2:47). These converted persons are Christ's church because they belong to Christ. However, in much of the past teaching in the church, it was assumed that the person who understood the necessity of being baptized automatically understood what it meant to belong to Christ. That is a false assumption. The essentiality of baptism in Scripture is shown easily to any sincere person wishing to understand. Many people do understand Scripture's teaching on baptism. Yet, many of these people do not understand the meaning of belonging to Christ. They were baptized because the Bible said do it, but they know little about belonging to Christ.

The essential question is not, "Must I be baptized?" It is, "Do I accept the Lordship of Christ?" Is He really Lord with all authority over the individual and the church? Is He the ruler of one's personal life and the church? Is He the sole authority over His people? Is the Word the only source for knowing and understanding the will of God? When a person sees and accepts the authoritative Lordship of Jesus, when he depends on the Word to show him the will of God, he wants both to be baptized and to belong to Jesus. He wants to *become* a Christian, not merely to acknowledge Jesus' identity.

Second, *too many Christians do not want to be converted people.* Unlike the Thessalonian Christians, they did not turn from lives of sin to serve the living God. Some did not turn at all. Their lives, their thoughts, and their emotions did not change. They retained their evil habits and pleasures. They have no intention of serving. "Belonging" to the church, not serving, is their concern. It is the fear of hell, not the desire to live with God, which motivates them.

Unlike the Christians of Rome, they did not obey the teachings from the heart. They obeyed because they feared the consequence of disobedience. The heart had little to do with their decision. They do not act like persons free from sin or bondservants of righteousness.

Unlike the prodigal, they never came to themselves. The prodigal knew he had to leave the pigpen. His conditions would change only if he got out of the pigpen and went to the father. *Too many Christians continue life in the foreign pigpen of sin and pleasure.* They want the Father to love them by saving them where they are, as they are. It cannot happen!

Christians must learn the difference between being converted and "belonging to the church." One must want more than hell insurance. He must want the Lordship of Jesus Christ.

## Questions
1. Name and describe common groups seen in any cause.
2. What two frightening situations have these groups produced in the Lord's church?
3. Explain this statement: too many Christians have been convinced but not converted.
4. Describe a "convinced" Christian. Why are some Christians content to be convinced?
5. Describe a "converted" Christian. Why does being converted hurt?
6. Why is being converted a life-shattering experience?
7. What moment of fear and despair is produced by being converted?
8. What is the relationship between being converted and finding a Savior?
9. Illustrate the process of conversion with these examples:
   a. The Thessalonian Christians
   b. The Christians at Rome
   c. The prodigal son
10. Can you suggest other examples of the conversion process?
11. What three things happen in conversion?

## Thought Questions
1. Why are many Christians spiritually apathetic?
2. How can a Scripturally baptized person determine if he is convinced or converted?
3. What do you personally consider the most important lesson in this chapter?

# Chapter Two

# Attitudes Toward Self

## *Part One*

"How should I look at me?" is a problem question most Christians find extremely difficult to answer. No one who has been a Christian long has escaped the intense personal struggle of deciding how to feel about self. It is an intimate, perplexing struggle which can be resolved by no one but the individual Christian.

Christians commonly feel guilty about the way they look at themselves. Occasionally a Christian will experience a deep sense of happiness and contentment because he feels good about his life. Such moments create a natural high and a deep sense of well-being. Yet, such moments frequently are followed by strong guilt feelings because he felt good about himself. He feels it is wrong to be happy with who and what he is because pride has triumphed over humility. In a feeling of uncertainty, he actually tries to eliminate any positive views of self. He reasons, "The Christian must know he is nothing and Christ is everything."

There are frequent moments when Christians look at themselves as being nothing. In these moments, they chide themselves, lecture themselves, condemn themselves, declare how terrible they have been, and confess how shamefully they have failed. Feeling depressed and miserable, they hold themselves in contempt. The result is horrible self-images which produce useless, nonproductive Christians. They are convinced they are spiritual failures who could not possibly be of value to Christ.

*It is essential that a Christian understand the proper spiritual attitudes which he should have toward himself.* First, if he does not understand the proper way to view himself, his spiritual frustration will produce spiritual inactivity and uselessness. Second, the way a Christian looks at himself powerfully influences the way he looks at God and Christ. The New Testament established two parameters which define the boundaries of Christians' attitudes toward self. This chapter is devoted to the first attitude.

## *Faith And Servitude*

Jesus gave the first parameter attitude in Luke 17:5–10:

> And the apostles said unto the Lord, Increase our faith. And the Lord said, If ye had faith as a grain of mustard seed, ye would say unto this sycamore tree, Be thou rooted up, and be thou planted in the sea; and it would obey you. But who is there of you having a servant plowing or keeping sheep, that will say unto him, when he is come in from the

field, Come straightway and sit down to meat; and will not rather say unto him, Make ready wherewith I may sup, and gird thyself, and serve me, till I have eaten and drunken; and afterward thou shalt eat and drink? Doth he thank the servant because he did the things that were commanded? Even so ye also, when ye shall have done all the things that are commanded you, say, We are unprofitable servants; we have done that which was our duty to do.

The context of this passage centers on two frightening responsibilities declared by Jesus (vv. 1–4). First, one must not cause others to stumble. It is better to drown in the sea with a millstone around one's neck than to cause another to stumble. The declaration that it is better to be killed than to discourage a person following Jesus is quite sobering. Obviously, no Christian lives for himself alone. He must be a constructive spiritual example for those who observe his life.

The second responsibility was that of forgiveness. One is to rebuke a sinful brother and to forgive a penitent brother. Forgiveness is difficult because (1) it is exercised only when one has been wronged, and (2) it demands one be spiritually mature in dealing with his own feelings and hurts. Jesus made it more demanding: if one is sinned against by the same person seven times in a day, and each time is asked for forgiveness, he is to forgive all seven times. Can there be a more difficult demand in human relationships?

The apostles reacted to these two responsibilities by saying, "Lord, increase our faith." They unquestionably understood the difficulty of both responsibilities. The only way they could be the example they must be and to forgive as they must was to have more faith. To their credit, rather than complaining about Jesus' expectations, they asked for the faith necessary to fulfill the responsibilities.

The text began with the request for faith. Jesus acknowledged that their faith was smaller than a tiny mustard seed. Though they had faith enough to leave personal involvements, families, and friends to follow Jesus unquestioningly on a daily basis, that did not equal a mustard seed.

It must be noted that the Twelve did not remain men of mustard seed faith. After the resurrection of Jesus and the establishment of the church, they became living and dying sacrifices for the Lord. They preached Christ and established congregations in hostile pagan communities. No obstacle or discouragement could hide the reality of Christ within their lives. In one generation they were directly responsible for preaching the gospel to the known world. Some of the better-organized persecution in history was powerless to stop them.

In the text, Jesus asked the Twelve a peculiar question. If they sent a bondservant out to plow or keep sheep, how would they treat him when he returned that evening? Would they have prepared his meal and cared for him? Or, would they instruct him to hurry and to prepare their meal? Would they thank the servant for doing what he was commanded and expected to do? The answers were self-evident in their society. The master never served the servant; the servant always served the master. When the servant worked hard, he had done nothing more than was expected and proper.

Jesus then made this obvious application to them: when they did everything commanded, they had done nothing more than was expected. Even in perfect obedience, they only would have fulfilled their rightful, basic responsibility. Even in complete obedience, they should consider themselves as unprofitable servants.

## Increasing Faith

What is the relationship between the apostles asking for more faith, Jesus acknowledging they needed more faith, and Jesus' lesson about the obedient servant? At first it seems to be a disjointed sequence of unrelated ideas. *The essence of faith is a keen awareness of total dependence on God.* To speak of faith is to talk about confidence or trust. The Apostles' request for increased faith was a request for increased confidence and trust in Him and God. They were asking Jesus to increase their level of dependence on Him. Faith exists to the degree that a person actually depends on God and Christ.

To increase personal faith, one must firmly understand who depends on whom. "Am I dependent on Christ or is He dependent on me? Am I God's source of security, or is He mine? Does God serve me, or do I serve God? Who is in the role of need and dependence, and who is in the role of power and sustainer?" A person can increase his trust in God only when he increases his awareness of the extent of his dependence on God.

For Jesus to increase their faith, they had to understand they were as responsible to God as a bondservant was to his master. They were not doing God a favor by learning not to be a stumbling block and to forgive. They were not making an extraordinary sacrifice; they were accepting their rightful responsibility. To grow in faith, they had to accept the servant's role of complete dependence and total servitude.

An "affirming" faith is easily developed. It is a declared faith primarily expressed by words. It demonstrates itself by saying, "I believe . . ." Such faith could not fulfill Jesus' expectations.

The faith of dependence is difficult to develop because it is a functioning faith. It places confidence and security in God through actions. It obeys, and it trusts promises. While it is not hesitant to say it believes, its trust does not stop with mere words.

*Growing faith is a dependent faith which knows the Lord cannot expect too much of His servants.* That faith knows even perfect obedience only has accepted rightful responsibility. Doing all one has the power to do is doing no more than what is rightfully expected. Obedience is not a monumental accomplishment; it is a Christian's basic responsibility.

## *Faith Or Arrogance?*

How do these thoughts relate to a Christian's attitude toward self? First, they are relevant because of the ease with which a serving, obedient Christian can develop attitudes of arrogance, of self-strength, and of self-dependence. His attitude can become, "Lord, you should be proud of me — look at all I do for you!" Or, "Lord, you might be able to do without me, but it would be hard." He thus reverses roles with Christ. Christ depends on him more than he depends on Christ. As self-dependence grows, faith diminishes. Ironically, *this person thinks he is growing in faith while his faith actually shrinks.*

Peter is the classic example of this problem. When Jesus foretold His death, Peter rebuked Him saying such was impossible (Matt. 16:21, 22). At the last supper when Jesus said the disciples would be scattered, Peter said he would never be offended (Matt. 26:31–35). In the garden, Peter did put his life on the line by defending Jesus with a sword. Yet, in all of this, Peter's confidence was not in Jesus. It was in Peter. He did not need for Jesus to take care of him. He was going to take care of Jesus. Prior to fleeing from the garden, this self-declared servant unto death would have professed great faith in Jesus. However, he neither had great faith nor was a true servant. Because confident Peter depended on himself rather than Jesus, he denied the Lord three times. His failure to be dependent dismantled his faith.

Second, the passage relates to attitudes toward self because it stresses Christians must not exaggerate the importance and significance of their service and obedience. The Apostles are an excellent example of this problem. Did they not argue over who was to be the greatest (Luke 9:46–48)? Were they not jealous about the seating around the throne (Mark 10:35–44)? Did they not ask, "Lord, what will be our reward since we left everything to follow you" (Matt. 19:27)? The Apostles held such attitudes because they attached great significance to their obedience and their following Jesus. *They forgot they were simply servants fulfilling their rightful responsibility.*

While every Christian should want to serve in the finest capacity and obey as fully as possible, no one should exaggerate the significance of his service and obedience. While God is deeply pleased with service and obedience, Christians never do more than they should do.

Third, the text relates to Christian attitudes toward self because of the ease with which Christians can feel abused or feel sorry for themselves. Christians can deceive themselves into believing that service and obedience give them a special bargaining power with God. Some Christians obey and serve to gain a bargaining advantage with the Lord or to acquire spiritual insurance against hardship. They expect protection against physical suffering and disaster. Guaranteed earthly happiness and security are expected. *When the inevitable sorrow, crisis, or hardship comes, this Christian feels betrayed.* The bargain has been broken; the Lord did not keep the agreement. Confident that they are victims of gross injustice, they feel abused and sorry for themselves. In their bewilderment, their faith is in jeopardy. These feelings and attitudes are as old as Job. Again, the person has forgotten he is dependent, he is the servant.

If a master sent a servant out to plow at sunrise, the servant would be expected to plow all day. If he plowed well accomplishing twice what was expected, the master would not say, "You did so well today, forget about plowing for a while." If plowing remained, he would be expected to do just as well the next day. If he plowed exceptionally the whole season, the master would not say, "You plowed so well this year, I will never ask you to plow again." Instead, the master would send him to plow each year expecting work well done. If the servant plowed well all his life, the master would be pleased and regard him as an exceptional servant. Even so, he would only have done the work of a servant. He accomplished only what was expected. No one would consider the master abusive because the servant was continually expected to do exceptional work.

*The attitude of great Christian faith begins with the awareness of total dependence on Jesus.* Each Christian must understand, "I do not feed, clothe, support, or sustain the Lord. He was not made King, Lord, and Savior by my hand or power. I came to Him. His position, power, and being are not dependent on me."

The first parameter Christian attitude toward self is this: "I am forever the Lord's servant. Though I shall serve with all my being to do the best of my ability, I am still a servant. I have only accepted my responsibility." Only the knowledge and admission of dependence will enable a Christian to grow in faith and in usefulness to the Lord.

## Questions

1. Explain why the question, "How should I look at me?" is a problem question.
2. Explain why some Christians feel guilty because they feel good about themselves.
3. Why must Christians have proper spiritual attitudes toward self?
4. Why did the Apostles ask Jesus to increase their faith in Luke

17:5? Discuss the difficult responsibilities Jesus had given them.
5. Explain Jesus' point in the illustration about the hard-working servant who had to prepare the master's supper before eating.
6. What must a person understand to increase his faith?
7. Describe an "affirming" faith.
8. Describe the faith of dependence.
9. What does a growing, dependent faith know?
10. Discuss how obedience can result in an arrogant attitude.
11. Discuss how obedience can result in a Christian exaggerating his importance.
12. Why is it easy for some Christians to feel abused?
13. What is the first parameter attitude of a Christian toward himself?

## Thought Questions

1. Give your own explanation of the importance of this attitude: "I am and forever shall be a servant to the Lord."
2. Why must a Christian have this attitude?
3. If a Christian does not have this attitude, what will be the consequences?
4. What do you consider to be the most important lesson in this chapter?

# Chapter Three

# Attitudes Toward Self

## Part Two

What effect did Jesus have on the first-century people who followed Him? Were his followers a group of depressed, anxious people who were down on life, down on themselves, and in general "a bunch of real losers"? Were they a bland, disinterested, unexcitable people with little feeling? Were they an optimistic, hopefilled group who possessed a purpose in life?

*The gospels make it evident that one never became less a person by following Jesus.* Being Jesus' disciple was not a debasing, degrading experience. Many rejected Jesus, refused faith in Him, and resented His teachings. However, those who followed Him came from every conceivable background composing an interesting cross section of first-century society. Among those who followed Him were the typical "average person", social rejects, prostitutes, despised tax collectors, religious radicals such as the Zealots, and even a few prestigious people. Did these followers consider themselves the world's great failures, the scum of the earth, or a worthless people of no significance? The gospels and Acts reveal such attitudes did not characterize Jesus' followers. They followed Jesus to escape guilt, not to find it; to destroy defeated lives, not to find defeat; to get away from purposelessness, not to produce it. Following Jesus made them persons of value, not miserable, beaten failures.

Jesus did not say, "Come unto me burdened, and I will increase your burdens. I will make you know how miserable and worthless you are. I will fill your lives with guilt, anxiety, and self-contempt." The life Jesus offered was based on a unique concept of self: a person alive in Jesus must respect himself because he is a child of God. This chapter is devoted to the second parameter attitude toward self: "I am God's child."

## God's Child

From Jesus' ministry onward, Scripture stressed each Christian was God's child. John wrote of Jesus,

> But as many as received him, to them gave he the right to become children of God, even to them that believe on His name: who were born, not of blood, nor of the will of the flesh, nor of the will of man, but of God. (John 1:12, 13)

The right to be God's child is dependent on receiving Jesus. An act of God makes a child of God out of each person who believes on Jesus and is born of God.

Caiaphas declared that it was expedient for Jesus to die to preserve the nation. Caiaphas did not comprehend the significance of his statement, but John wrote,

> Now this he said not of himself: but being high priest that year, he prophesied that Jesus should die for the nation; and not for the nation only, but that He might also gather together into one the children of God that are scattered abroad. (John 11:51, 52)

The idea that Jesus died to gather into one the children of God was new to first-century thinking. Becoming God's children was a new emphasis. While the Jews considered themselves God's people, their common emphasis stressed their being descendants of Abraham. Though God had long prophesied He would create His family from all peoples (Hosea 2:23 with Romans 9:25, 26; Romans 15:8–12 with corollary Old Testament references), the fact that God's family was not to be limited to the Jews was new to their thinking. The universal family of God would come into existence because Jesus would die for the people.

After Jesus' death, all who entered into Christ became sons of God. Paul wrote, "For ye are all sons of God, through faith, in Christ Jesus. For as many of you as were baptized into Christ did put on Christ" (Galatians 3:26, 27). Faith combined with being in Christ produced sons of God. The moment they were baptized into Christ they became sons of God.

No passage more beautifully emphasized the reality of God's family than I John 3:1–3.

> Behold what manner of love the Father hath bestowed upon us, that we should be called children of God; and such we are. For this cause the world knoweth us not, because it knew him not. Beloved, now are we children of God, and it is not yet made manifest what we shall be. We know that, if he shall be manifested, we shall be like Him; for we shall see Him even as he is. And everyone that hath this hope set on him purifieth himself, even as he is pure.

The Greek language stressed two things in verse one. "Behold, what manner of love" is written to express astonishment. John said, "Let me show you an incredible fact about God's love", or, "Let me reveal a fact about God's love so astounding it is virtually unthinkable." "That we should be called children of God" is written in a verb tense to emphasize a present, real, continuing fact. Being called God's children is not a pleasant thought or an inspiring idea. *Divine sonship is an accomplished, continuing fact.* Apart from the Greek, this incredible act of divine love is evident. How could God look upon beings He created as His own children? That is precisely what God did, and it is an act of love which defies comprehension. Elevating Christians to the status of His own children was not a symbolic act, a meaningful gesture, or the conferring of an honorary title. In actual relationship Christians became His children, brothers and sisters of Jesus in the same divine family.

God will yet accomplish something more astounding than making Christians His children. What is yet to come for those who are God's children is beyond explanation or description. This second great act of God can be understood vaguely in this: when Christ returns, Christians shall be as He is. The hope of that glory, privilege, and existence is a basic motivation for Christian living. The desire to be a part of God's eternal family in heaven causes the Christian to devote himself to purity with Jesus as the standard.

## *The Value of Sonship*

The second parameter attitude of a Christian toward self is based on the understanding that God valued his life so much He made him His child. *The privilege of salvation is sonship with God.* A Christian is not a created "thing" to God. He is not an impersonal "something" to be used and discarded. He is not a possession to God. In the slave-master world of the first century, slaves were possessions valued for their service. Masters cared for their slaves not out of concern for their well-being but as a matter of good business in protecting their investment. God does not and never has regarded Christians as pieces of property which have value only to the extent that they can render productive work.

The New Testament abounds with evidence of the Christians' value to God as His family. God so valued Christians that He sent His Son from heaven, let Him be born as the creature He helped create, let Him be a true man on earth, and committed Him to death. God let Jesus die only because He valued those people who would accept Jesus' sacrifice. Jesus valued Christians so much that He accepted and completed that mission. He did so only because He valued those who would come to Him in faith and obedience.

One of the most powerful, encouraging promises ever given Christians is Romans 8:31–39. Paul declared to all those who continue in Christ that God is for them. He is on their side. He cannot lose interest in them nor desert them. No power in heaven, on earth, or in hell can separate the believing, trusting Christian from Christ's love. *Nothing outside of the Christian himself has the power to come between the Christian and Jesus' love.* The foundation of that assurance is the fact of Jesus' death. If God valued the Christian to the extent that He did not hesitate to allow Jesus to be sacrificed cruelly on the cross, God will not refuse those things necessary for the Christian's spiritual needs and spiritual well-being. Because of the value God places on the Christian, because of the sacrifice God made for the Christian, and because of God's determination to sustain the Christian, the Christian is more than conqueror through the loving Savior.

Ephesians 3:20 affirmed God can do "exceedingly abundantly above all that we ask or think, according to the power that worketh in us." The Christian cannot "out need" the available power of God to help him. God's options to aid are not limited to the Christian's imagination.

Peter wrote to persecuted, oppressed Christians, ". . . casting all your anxiety upon Him (God), because He careth for you" (I Peter 5:7). God will readily accept a Christian's anxiety and bear it Himself. The concerns and stresses falling upon His children matter to Him. That which distresses His children is of personal concern to Him.

To whom are such definite, absolute commitments made? No one makes such promises to worthless, meaningless people. Only to those who are valued are such powerful promises made. God's promises are irrefutable evidence of the value He places on each Christian.

*If a Christian understands the value God places on him, he must respect himself in Christ.* Christ wants no Christian to feel negative about himself, to be doubtridden about his life, or to be convinced he is good for nothing. He must understand, "Jesus wants me to be filled with spirit and drive, with confidence and determination, and with the conviction that He has made me useful and worthwhile."

## Servitude And Sonship

The two parameter attitudes of a Christian toward self are (1) "I am Jesus Christ's servant who exists to serve Him to the best of my ability," and (2) "I am a child of God, and I will be loved and valued as a child as long as I live in Christ." At first glance, these attitudes seem to be in contradiction. How can one be both a servant and a son? Does servitude destroy sonship? Does sonship release one from the responsibility of servitude? To properly understand these two attitudes, one must separate two basic realities. Reality one: each Christian has a *responsibility* to God. Reality two: each Christian has a *relationship* with God. A Christian cannot have the right attitude toward himself unless he separates the awareness of responsibility from the awareness of relationship.

*A Christian's responsibility to God is that of a servant.* At great personal cost and sacrifice, God reached down into the filth of sin when the person was spiritually dead and freed him from death by cleansing his life. Jesus literally bought him back from the condemnation of sin with His own blood. Nothing he can do can repay God and Jesus for what They did. He can give no sacrifice that would made it worth Their effort, and he can perform no act to equal Their deeds in providing salvation. Being a devoted servant to the will of God and using all of life to render faithful service is the only way he can return Their love.

*A Christian's relationship with God is that of a child with a loving father.* God loves him, values him, and holds him as precious. As long as he lives in the Son, no physical or spiritual force can make him less than a loved, valued, appreciated child. He derives his identity and dignity from sonship with God. He can respect himself because God in Christ made him respectable by applying the righteousness of Jesus to his life. In Christ he is somebody! He has the blessing of self-respect, dignity, and unquenchable hope because God created him anew in Jesus.

God expects two things of a Christian in his attitude toward self. The Christian must not be a person of arrogance, pride, and high-mindedness who considers himself an equal or peer to God. He must not exaggerate his significance and importance nor feel too good nor too important to serve. Neither must the Christian be filled with self-contempt, guilt, and doubt. God did not make him a child for him to debase himself, to feel useless, to feel worthless, or to believe he is valueless. Both of these attitudes are equally wrong, equally sinful, and equally unchristian.

Throughout life a Christian asks himself two questions: "What does God expect of me? How much does God value me?" He must understand the answers to both questions. God expects him to serve Him with all the power of his being. God wants him never to forget he is His child.


## Questions

1. What effect did Jesus have on the people who followed him?
2. Why did people follow Jesus?
3. What is the second parameter attitude a Christian has toward himself?
4. Explain what each of the following passages teaches about being a child of God:
   a. John 1:12, 13
   b. John 11:51, 52
   c. Galatians 3:26, 27
   d. I John 3:1–3
5. What is the privilege of salvation in Christ? Discuss the meaning of the fact.
6. What does Romans 8:31–39 teach about the value of a Christian to God?
7. Use Ephesians 3:20 to explain why a Christian cannot "out need" God's available power.
8. How does I Peter 5:7 emphasize God's care for Christians?
9. When a Christian understands how much God values him, what fact must he accept?

10. Carefully explain how a Christian can see himself as a servant and as a son at the same time.
11. What are God's two basic expectations of each Christian in regard to his attitudes toward himself?
12. As a Christian walks through life, what two questions must he ask and answer?

## *Thought Questions*

1. What happens in a Christian's life when he fully understands he is God's servant but does not understand he is God's child?
2. What happens in a Christian's life when he fully understands he is God's child but does not understand he is God's servant?
3. What do you regard as the most important lesson in this chapter?

**Chapter Four**

# How Do You Solve Troubles?

Everyone is convinced he has more than his share of troubles. Most people readily will talk about having many problems. Yet, most people are hesitant to discuss specific problems because they fear they will reveal the depth of their struggles. The Christian does not exist who does not struggle with some spiritual matters, who does not fight internal battles, and who does not have some problem that he fears is unresolvable. Every Christian wearies of his own conflicts. Since personal troubles create a continuing, daily dilemma for every Christian, how should he seek to solve troubles and problems?

### *Attitudes Toward Troubles*

No Christian responsibility exceeds the challenge of developing the proper outlook on problems. The variety of attitudes concerning problems held by Christians illustrates the difficulty. *Attitude one: "Ignore troubles!"* One is to pretend troubles are not there and act as though they do not exist. He is to refuse to think about them or to consider their effects. However, few people have the ability to ignore personal troubles even briefly. Those who can ignore them can do so only temporarily. One cannot pretend troubles away. Troubles exist because something is amiss in one's life, and that something is serious enough to cause pain and frustration. Ignoring troubles only allows them to grow in size and seriousness.

*Attitude two: "Give in to troubles."* This is a defeatist's attitude of surrender. He reasons he cannot win against troubles for three reasons: they are bigger than he is; he cannot destroy them; and they will never cease. Fighting against them only produces pain and a prolonged struggle. His philosophy is to choose the course of the least amount of suffering. It guarantees he will encounter serious depression which likely will end in despair.

*Attitude three: "Accept troubles as a fact and learn to live with them."* This is likely the most common Christian attitude toward personal troubles. It is the most common advice given to those struggling with problems. This advice declares one is to accept his troubles by refusing to ignore them or to pretend the troubles are not there. Under no circumstances does he surrender to them. After making necessary adjustments, he lives his life in spite of his troubles. While this attitude contains definite elements of a healthy spiritual outlook, it does not answer some important questions. Is a

Christian's only recourse to live with his troubles? Is the only answer to all troubles accepting them and making necessary adjustments?

*Attitude four: "Destroy your troubles by solving them."* Every Christian would agree that this attitude is a worthy ambition and a noble aspiration. Yet, everyone knows the difficulty of actually resolving all troubles. A few years of adulthood teaches one that some problems defy solution regardless of one's determination or good intentions.

## Troubles And Solutions

While "solve your problems" would be the obvious attitude of choice, the question remains, "How do you solve personal troubles?" Will determination and effort solve all problems? Can a Christian realistically hope to eliminate all his troubles by resolving them? No! Regardless of his faith and determination, a Christian cannot solve all his personal troubles for two reasons. *First, some troubles exist because of the deeds, actions, or troubles of others.* If the trouble in part or in whole is produced by someone else, complete resolution of the problem does not lie in one's own power. He is not helpless and powerless in the face of such troubles. He simply cannot resolve them alone.

*Second, some private troubles are beyond an individual's power to resolve.* 2 Corinthians 12:7–10 illustrates this truth in Paul's life:

> By reason of the exceeding greatness of the revelations, that I should not be exalted overmuch, there was given to me a thorn in the flesh, a messenger of Satan to buffet me, that I should not be exalted overmuch. Concerning this thing I besought the Lord thrice, that it might depart from me. And he hath said unto me, My grace is sufficient for thee: for my power is made perfect in weakness. Most gladly therefore will I rather glory in my weaknesses, that the power of Christ may rest upon me. Wherefore I take pleasure in weaknesses, in injuries, in necessities, in persecutions, in distresses, for Christ's sake: for when I am weak then am I strong.

To guard Paul against conceit, he received, suffered from, and endured a thorn in the flesh sent from Satan. The Lord refused to remove the problem. He declared His grace would sustain Paul, and His power would be perfected in Paul's weakness. With that understanding, Paul accepted his problem as a blessing rather than a frustration.

*Were it not for troubles, Christians would be self-reliant and would be convinced that they did not need the Lord's help.* Even with troubles they too easily become self-reliant. Some troubles are in the Christian's best spiritual interest because they serve as a constant reminder of his need for and dependence upon the Lord's strength. Continuing troubles cause Christians to understand that the true power of spiritual preservation and endurance is found in total dependence upon the Lord.

What personal troubles can a Christian resolve? Basically he can resolve those which are of his own making. Those include troubles which exist because of one's own actions, of personal feelings and attitudes, of ignorance, and of one's own lack of wisdom and spirituality. These are the common sources of most personal troubles and of most of life's hurts and pains.

## Hindering Solution

To solve personal troubles, one must understand the factors which prohibit a solution. Some attitudes and actions make it impossible for a person to solve his troubles. Those actions and attitudes must be identified and understood. To live with troubles which can be resolved is foolish and destructive. A Christian must be certain his troubles are not continuing because he stands in the way of the solution.

*First, a Christian can prohibit a solution to his troubles by defending the faults and weaknesses which produced the problem.* Most troubles exist for one of two reasons. He refuses to identify his faults and weaknesses, or he defends his faults or weaknesses by arguing that they are innocent and not responsible for the problem. Some Christians are actually proud of their faults and weaknesses saying, "I am not ashamed that I . . . It is foolish and ridiculous for anyone to think that is harmful." This turns the faults and weaknesses which created the troubles into personal merits. Troubles are never resolved by defending faults and weaknesses.

*Second, a Christian can prohibit a solution to his troubles by justifying his mistakes, faults, or weaknesses.* Common justifications include these: "I know this is wrong; I should not act this way; I should not have this attitude. But the situation is not really my fault; I am not to blame." "If brother Joe had not acted as he did, I would never have done that." "The circumstances gave me no other choice." Often when a troubled Christian is encouraged to accept responsibility for his actions, he responds, "I am certain in the same situation you would have done the same thing — or worse!" Or, "You were not there and do not understand; had you been there, you would not say that!" The reasoning which justifies one's weaknesses is this: (1) What was done was undeniably wrong. (2) However, a reason makes it right in my situation. (3) Circumstances demand that it should be ignored in my case. (4) My situation is an exception. Troubles are never resolved by justifying or excusing weaknesses.

*Third, a Christian can prohibit a solution to his troubles by evading or ignoring faults and weaknesses.* This person emphatically declares there is nothing wrong with him, and he has done nothing wrong. The personal problem exists, but it is not the result of his actions. Or, this person adeptly ignores the trouble by refusing to talk about it. By choosing to ignore the whole matter he declares it is no one's concern but his. In either case, the person is pretending. The idea of his having a problem is a creation of someone else's imagination. Troubles are never resolved by evading or ignoring mistakes or weaknesses.

## Aiding Solution

To solve personal problems, one also must understand the factors which aid a solution. *First, he must admit the problem is there.* As an example, an alcoholic and a drug addict cannot be helped until they admit their addiction. Both commonly refuse to admit their addiction. They pretend they have a smaller, more manageable problem. This attitude is characteristic of all problemed people including Christians. It is hard to confess problems to self. The problem itself generates an intimidating fear which forces the person to hide from himself. Confessing the problem is confessing a failure; no one wishes to admit failure. Confessing the problem is an admission that one cannot cope with the problem; that is a distasteful admission.

*Second, he must look for the source of the trouble within himself.* The Christian with the courage and honesty to admit his troubles arise from his own life is rare. Most will blame any possible thing to create a scapegoat and to evade the responsibility and failure. Rather than admit the cause lies within their own minds and hearts, they play the role of the victim. Christians who are serious about resolving troubles must ask themselves some hard questions and search for honest answers within.

*Third, he must have a "gut desire" to either defeat the problem or control the trouble.* Wanting the trouble to end or preferring the problem to be resolved is insufficient. Only a compelling desire which makes finding a solution a  matter of urgency and of top priority will create sufficient motivation to produce change. Changing has to become a *must.*

Christians who use troubles for a convenient excuse for their actions and behavior do not want their troubles to disappear. Neither do those who use their troubles to evade spiritual responsibility or service. Their professions of desiring solutions are often less than honest.

## The Critical Factor

*The greatest factor in coping with or triumphing over personal troubles is confidence in the Lord's ability to help His people.* The Christian who is determined to resolve his troubles will lay aside all defenses, excuses, false justifications, evasions, and pretenses. He will pray, "Lord, please help me. I hold nothing back; I ask without reservation or qualification. Help me! In any way You can, with whatever it takes, help me!"

It is easy to say, "Lord, help me!" This usually means, "Lord, use Your power in some marvelous way to make my troubles disappear." This person sits as a bystander awaiting a wondrous act which never comes. It is more difficult to say, "Lord, help me! I hold nothing back." This person is ready to do anything, to make any change if granted the wisdom to understand what to do. This good attitude is still not the spiritually mature attitude. The most difficult statement is, "Lord, with no reservations or qualifications, I ask You to help me in any way You will." This person makes no conditions, places nothing off-limits. There are no restrictions on how God helps or what experiences he must endure. He seeks help regardless of what must happen. This is the attitude of mature faith which builds solutions.

When a Christian asks for God's help with troubles or problems, he is requesting one of the following: (1) He is asking God to resolve the problem through a solution which will end the matter. (2) If a solution is not possible, he is asking God for the wisdom and understanding to cope with the problem. Coping allows him through Christ to retain control of his life. (3) If coping is not possible, he is asking God for the strength to endure the problem. Though he cannot control the problem, the strength enables him to live through it. He still chooses the life in Christ he wants and keeps his faith and hope intact. When a Christian has full faith in God, he is confident God can do any of these three things. He does not choose which of the three God must do; he gratefully accepts any of the three.

*The critical issue in resolving troubles is faith.* Faith is measured by the degree one trusts the Lord. On a night filled with more troubles than any Christian today could imagine, Jesus tried to prepare his best friends for his betrayal and execution. Revealing the unthinkable, he declared he would be killed, and he would go to a place they could not come. They would be scattered and come to be hated and rejected. All that the disciples could see were troubles crashing down upon them. In those moments of uncertainty and confusion, Jesus said, "Let not your heart be troubled; believe in God; believe also in me" (John 14:1). Moments later he said, "These things have I spoken unto you, that in me ye may have peace. In the world ye have tribulation: but be of good cheer; I have overcome the world" (John 16:33). Tribulations are unavoidable in this world. Even so, in Him there is peace.

Years after witnessing that night, Peter wrote, "Humble yourselves therefore under the mighty hand of God, that he may exalt you in due time; casting all your anxiety upon him, for he careth for you" (I Peter 5:6, 7). Paul, who knew the full meaning of trouble, wrote, "In nothing be anxious; but in everything by prayer and supplication with thanksgiving let your requests be made known unto God" (Philippians 4:6). Again, he wrote, "Now unto him that is able to do exceeding abundantly above all that we ask or think, according to the power that worketh in us, unto him be the glory in the church and in Christ Jesus unto all generations for ever and ever. Amen." (Ephesians 3:20, 21)

*There is nothing in life so terrible or so powerful that it surpasses the Lord's ability to help His people.* The Lord can help a Christian with any form of trouble or any kind of problem. Nothing is beyond His helping and caring. Being helped with troubles is never a question of the Lord's power. It is a question of trusting the Lord's power, of being honest and open about one's troubles, and of being willing to pay faith's price of solving, coping with, or enduring one's troubles. Because Jesus has overcome the world, He can help any Christian overcome. If one believes in God and in Jesus, he has no reason to let his heart be troubled.

## Questions

1. Name and explain four common attitudes toward problems.
2. Explain why ignoring problems cannot solve problems.
3. Why should people not "give in" to their problems?
4. Why is accepting one's troubles an inadequate approach to problems?
5. What is the basic difficulty with the attitude which declares that all problems should be solved?
6. Can any Christian resolve all problems and thus eliminate them from his life? Explain your answer.
7. What would be the result if Christians had no troubles?
8. Explain how each of the following factors prohibits solutions to problems:
    a. Defending one's faults and weaknesses
    b. Excusing or justifying one's faults, mistakes, or weaknesses
    c. Evading or ignoring mistakes, faults, or weaknesses
9. Explain the importance of each of the following factors in solving troubles:
    a. Admitting the trouble is there
    b. Looking within one's self for the true source of the trouble
    c. The overpowering desire to control the problem
10. Discuss the significance and effectiveness of the following pleas:
    a. "Lord, help me."
    b. "Lord, help me! I hold nothing back."
    c. "Lord, I ask you to help me without qualification or reservation."
11. A Christian is asking God to do one of three things when he asks God to resolve his problems. Give each and discuss it.

## Thought Questions

1. It is easy to pray for solutions for problems. Why is it hard to pray sincerely for God to help one to cope with a problem or to endure a trouble?
2. Why must a Christian know nothing in life is so terrible or so powerful that it surpasses the Lord's ability to help him?
3. Discuss the blessings to be found in facing problems or troubles.
4. What is the most important lesson in this chapter?

## Chapter Five

# Christian Self-Evaluation

How would you describe yourself as a person? What good exists in your life? What are your major shortcomings and your significant accomplishments? How would you describe yourself as a Christian? What spiritual good exists in your life? What are your major spiritual shortcomings and your significant spiritual accomplishments?

Is your evaluation of yourself as a person and as a Christian two different, distinct evaluations? If they overlap and entwine, how much do they overlap? Is what you are as a person and what you are as a Christian so entwined that an evaluation of one is an evaluation of both?

Self-evaluation is an inescapable process in everyone's life. Some seek to eliminate self-evaluation by ignoring it, by hiding from it, or by pretending they never do it. Others abuse self-evaluation by using it as a means of self-glorification to arrogantly inflate their egos or by using considerable self-deceit in making evaluations. Though some seek to eliminate it and others abuse it, self-evalution is practiced by all. It is essential that Christians learn to practice it correctly.

## *The Responsibility To Evaluate*

Self-evaluation is a continuing responsibility for every Christian. In Galatians 6:3, 4 Paul wrote,

> For if a man thinketh himself to be something when he is nothing, he deceiveth himself. But let each man prove his own work, and then shall he have his glorying in regard of himself alone, and not of his neighbor.

The responsibility to "prove your own work" is the responsibility to evaluate one's own deeds and actions. Each Christian is to find his spiritual fulfillment and sense of accomplishment in Christ in terms of his own service to the Lord. One dare not build his spiritual sense of accomplishment on the labors of others.

Everyone enjoys being a member of an active, serving, working, achieving congregation. Many enjoy being around the activity without being a part of it. As they passively enjoy the activity and enthusiasm, they love to talk about what "we" are doing. Their whole sense of fulfillment and achievement is derived from the work of other Christians. Christians must protect themselves from this temptation by examining and evaluating their own involvements and services.

Why must a Christian practice self-evalution? *Self-evaluation protects the Christian from thinking he is something when he is nothing.* It is an essential protection against self-deceit. A Christian can lie to himself about himself more convincingly than he can lie to anyone else about anything else.

2 Corinthians 13:5 also emphasized the responsibility of self-evaluation. A segment of the Corinthian congregation attacked Paul and his work by denying his apostleship, discrediting his work, and attacking him as a person. Paul wrote that when he returned the matter would be resolved completely. Until that time, he instructed, "Try your own selves, whether ye are in the faith; prove your own selves."

In seeking to understand and declare God's truth, there is an enormous temptation to focus all attention on the lives and shortcomings of other people. It is easy for the Christian to become the expert who knows everyone else's sins and shortcomings but who never examines his own. Paul emphasized two continuing responsibilities each Christian must accept. First, he must try himself to see if he is in the faith. Second, he must prove or evaluate himself. This is not a once-in-a-lifetime nor even a once-a-year responsibility. It cannot be done when one occasionally takes a convenient break from evaluating everyone else. *The Christian's first responsibility in making evaluations is to himself.* His salvation does not hinge on being an expert in evaluating the lives of others; it depends on ably, honestly evaluating his own life.

I Corinthians 11:28 also stressed the responsibility of self-evaluation. Observance of the Lord's Supper was abused terribly in the Corinthian church. It had been perverted to the extent that Paul would not recognize it as an observance of the Supper. After specifying their abuses, Paul instructed them in the proper observance of the Lord's death and resurrection. In explaining the correct manner to commune, he stressed the seriousness of the observance. "But let a man prove himself, and so let him eat of the bread and drink of the cup."

*Self-evaluation is an essential part of proper observance of the Lord's Supper.* In communion the Christian seriously concentrates on two things: the death of Jesus and his own life. "Proving one's self" is not to see if one is worthy to take communion. In the true sense, no one is worthy because no Christian is deserving of Jesus' sacrifice. No human act can make one deserving. Nor is the purpose of the evaluation to determine if one is righteous or sinless enough to take communion. In taking communion this is never the issue because such righteousness and sinlessness is an impossibility. One proves himself by looking at who he is, what he has done, and how he is living. By considering the enormous sacrifice made by

God and Jesus, he sees and acknowledges his debt by standing squarely before it. This is the purpose of the evaluation. As a result, he is filled with gratitude, and he renews his determination to be more like the Savior who died for him.

Galatians 6:3, 4; 2 Corinthians 13:5; and I Corinthians 11:28 make it evident that Christian self-evaluation is essential to Christian existence.

## *The Responsibilities of Evaluating*

Christian self-evaluation contains three basic responsibilities. *First, he must know his own heart.* This requires him to know and understand his own feelings and motives. Is he following the Lord because of what he feels for Christ within his own heart, or is he merely going through the motions by observing meaningless habits?

*Second, the Christian must know his own influence.* He must examine the impact of his life on other people: mate, children, parents, co-workers, friends, neighbors, and associates. He needs to determine if his influence is leading others further from God or closer to the Lord. Every Christian is a living advertisement of the Lord's power to help His people. Can others see in him what Christ can do for a person? By observing him, are others convinced that the only distinguishable difference between those who are Christians and those who are not is a name?

*Third, he must know his own deeds.* He must ask, "What am I actually doing for the Lord? Am I spiritually productive? Do my deeds bless my Lord, or are they hurtful to Him and His cause?"

These three responsibilities are not an attempt to cultivate a good opinion of oneself. They are the responsibility to examine accurately one's life.

The responsibility of self-evaluation destroys the old myth that it is the preacher's job to evaluate people's lives. For generations too many Christians have believed it was the preacher's responsibility to "get on" people, to condemn people, and to tell people all about their sins. The common concept of a "good" preacher is the preacher who rides people who are wrong, stirs up people's guilt, and verbally flogs people for wayward living. Because of this myth many people define "good preaching" as preaching which walks roughshod over people and makes them feel guilty. While a legitimate part of preaching is opposing sin, it has never been the preacher's responsibility to preside as the official evaluator of the lives of the flock.

No one else has that responsibility. While elders watch in concern for the souls of members, they are no one's official evaluator. Nor is it the job of the family, the spouse, or the children. *Each Christian bears the primary responsibility for evaluating his own life.*

The Lord holds the individual responsible for making correct self-evaluation.

Self-evaluation is as difficult as it is necessary. They who believe self-evaluation is easy guarantee they will do a poor job of it. It is not effortless, and no one has a natural ability for it. Effective self-evaluation is dependent upon earnestness and sincerity.

*Accurate self-evaluation requires accurate knowledge of God's Word.* Evaluation is dependent upon a reliable standard of measurement. Accurate measurement of anything is dependent upon a reliable, known, available standard. Christian hearts and deeds are no different. If a Christian is ignorant of the proper standard, he will make the wrong evaluation of his life.

False standards for self-evaluation abound. More people use false standards than use God's Word. False standards include comparing oneself to the weak and unlearned; comparing oneself to spiritual failures who have reverted to sin; and comparing oneself to sinners who make no pretense of being godly. All such comparisons are meaningless and futile. Paul said, "They themselves, measuring themselves by themselves, and comparing themselves with themselves, are without understanding" (2 Corinthians 10:12). The lives of others can encourage a Christian, teach him, and help him gain understanding. However, the only proper standard for evaluating one's life is God's Word. Without understanding of the Word, an honest evaluation cannot be made.

*Accurate self-evaluation requires life's most difficult form of honesty.* One must be honest about the way he is living, what he is doing, and what he is not doing. He must be honest about his feelings, his attitudes, and his abilities. Life's most difficult form of honesty is honesty with self about self.

The reason for self-evaluation must be understood clearly. It is not an attempt to force an admission of mistakes. Admission of wrong is not the basic objective of self-evaluation. Developing humility is not the purpose. *Correction, not confession, is the purpose of self-evaluation.* One evaluates to correct attitudes, feelings, and deeds which are wrong. The objective is growth. Spiritual growth is possible when one understands the need to grow and identifies areas in which he must grow.

## Basic Awarenesses

As they evaluate, Christians must hold specific basic awarenesses. *Awareness one: "God measures me by me, and that is what I must do."* God's expectations for any person are based on his actual ability and potential. Divine expectations of an individual are never founded on the abilities of others. Jesus taught that God's expectations of a person are based on his true ability, true potential, and real opportunities. In the parable of the talents, the responsibility given each servant was based on his ability (Matthew 25:14–30). Each was judged on the basis of what he did with his ability. The two who used their opportunity to the best of their ability received precisely the same reward. Though one achieved more than the other, each was equally faithful in using his ability. A Christian must measure his spirituality by what he has the ability to be and by what he has the opportunity to do. He seeks to be 100% himself in Christ.

*Awareness two: the attitude, "I am as good as he is," is pointless and meaningless.* How good or bad someone else is has no bearing on God's evaluation of a Christian's faithfulness or service. If a sinner proves his daily life is as good as a Christian friend's, he does not thereby remove one sin. If a Christian proves he is as good as another Christian, he does not thereby make himself righteous or faithful in God's sight. To seek to prove one's goodness by comparisons to others is an attempt to "get by" or to "coast along." No spiritual state of "getting by" or "coasting along" exists.

*Awareness three: a Christian must understand he "proves himself" (1) to prevent self-deceit, (2) to avoid blindness, and (3) to increase personal spiritual productiveness.* One does not want to tell himself, "I am a growing Christian!" when he is spiritually sick and dying. He does not want to be blind to his real condition as was the church at Laodicea (Revelation 3:14–22). He wants to be increasingly fruitful, and not to be a branch to be pruned (John 15:1, 2).

The Christian who depends on a preacher to make him feel guilty is evading the responsibility of self-evaluation. If the preacher succeeds, it has little lasting effect or influence. However, when a Christian is motivated to evaluate his own life and to see for himself the changes he needs to make, lasting good is accomplished. The only person who can put a Christian's life in order is the Christian himself. Putting one's life in order must begin with self-evaluation.

## Questions
1. What is self-evaluation?
2. Read Galatians 6:3, 4.
   a. What is the meaning of "prove your own work"?
   b. Explain how Christians can build their sense of spiritual fulfillment on the labors of others.
   c. What is the fundamental reason for a Christian "proving his own work"?
3. Why did Paul tell the Corinthians to "try your own selves . . ., prove your own selves" (2 Corinthians 13:5)?
4. Explain the relationship between proper observance of the Lord's Supper and self-evaluation (1 Corinthians 11:28).
5. Explain the responsibility to know one's own heart.
6. Explain the responsibility to know one's influence.

7. Discuss the responsibility of knowing one's own deeds.
8. What myth have Christians long held concerning preachers?
9. What is the relationship between knowledge of the Word and accurate self-evaluation?
10. What is and is not the purpose of self-evaluation?
11. State and discuss the three basic awarenesses a Christian must have as he evaluates his life.

## *Thought Questions*

1. Why are Christians often fearful of making self-evaluations?
2. Why is self-evaluation essential to spiritual growth and Christian maturity?
3. Explain this statement: Christians cannot get to heaven by knowing the sins of others.
4. What is the most important lesson in this chapter?

# Chapter Six

# Christian Conduct: The Third Question

Consciously or unconsciously, every person determines how he will act and speak. Every knowledgeable Christian readily admits his God-given responsibility to govern and to control his speech and actions. Any sincere Christian openly will acknowledge he *must* accept that responsibility. Sincere Christians agree that what they say and do is of concern to the Lord and affects their spiritual well-being. The basic question for every Christian is this: "How do I decide how I should act and speak?"

The answers given to this question by any group of Christians are predictable. The majority would answer: "A Christian must determine what is wrong and then refuse to act and speak in that manner." A large number would answer: "A Christian must determine what is right and then act and speak in that manner." A few perceptive Christians would answer: "A Christian must determine both what is right and wrong, and then he must refuse to do the wrong and conscientiously do the right." Virtually all Christians would feel that the question had been answered properly with one of these answers.

Unquestionably Christians must determine what is wrong. It is equally necessary for them to determine what is right. As needful as it is to know right and wrong, only determining right and wrong is insufficient to determine proper Christian conduct. A third questions must be asked and answered: "What influence will my conduct and speech have?" By ignoring or forgetting this question, Christians have produced some major, hurtful spiritual problems.

## An Essential Question

The common neglect of the question of influence is easily illustrated. Most Christians feel their lives are spiritually sound if they determine, "Is it wrong?" To declare, "I see nothing wrong with it," is a common, accepted defense of actions, involvements, and speech. The Christian who asks, "Is it right?" is regarded as being unusually conscientious. Basing conduct on a determination of what is right is regarded as a mark of exceptional spiritual maturity. How many Christians regularly ask, "How will this affect my spiritual influence?" Compared to those who ask, "Is it wrong?" or, "Is it right?" they are few. Christians who regulate conduct on the basis of influence are regarded as being extreme, radical, and beyond being understood. *The question of influence has never been regarded as a necessary question.*

The New Testament forcefully emphasizes that Christians individually and collectively are to be concerned continuously about their influence. Christians are godly, honorable people who always want it to be evident that they are godly, honorable people. Paul made practical application of faith to daily life in Romans 12. In one application he said, "Take thought for things honorable in the sight of all men" (v. 17). Being honorable in everyone's sight is never accidental. Such influence is produced by careful thought about all of one's conduct in all of one's life. *The Christian who seeks to be honorable is concerned about everyone's thinking.* He even wants to be undeniably honorable before those who disapprove of his spiritual values and commitments. An honorable life is built by giving considerable thought to how one lives each day.

When distressed churches in Judea were in grave need, Gentile Christians provided financial relief. Read 2 Corinthians 8:16–24 and note the preparations made for delivering the gift. Though Paul was a self-sacrificing Apostle respected by many, he refused to place his reputation in the hands of chance. Caring for other's money easily can destroy one's reputation and influence. The absence of banks and international means of exchange meant the collection had to be carried several hundred miles to Judea. It is implied that each contributing congregation sent a representative with the gift. Additionally, a widely respected brother accompanied the group. This was not done because Paul was dishonest or because he did not trust himself. These were precautions to eliminate any opportunity for confusion, doubt, or unjust accusation. Nothing would destroy the good influence and the expression of love created by the gift. In Paul's words, ". . . We take thought for things honorable, not only in the sight of the Lord, but also in the sight of men" (v. 21). *Concern for doing things honorably in God's sight was insufficient.* Doing things honorably in the sight of people was equally important.

The difficult cultural and spiritual backgrounds of Jews and Gentiles created a difficult, sensitive problem in many first-century congregations. Congregations composed of both converts faced some delicate problems. Food created one such problem. The Gentiles always had eaten food offered to idols. Idolatrous festival days commonly were observed with a feast. The gifts of food were too numerous to be consumed on the festival day, and there was no way of preserving the foodstuffs. The surplus food was sold in the markets. The Gentiles were accustomed to eating at the feasts, to buying the surplus food, and to eating any kind of meat. The Jews by Mosaical command (Leviticus 11) had followed a strict dietary code which excluded many meats. They also believed eating food which had been offered to an idol honored a false god. For both reasons they vigorously refused to eat such food.

Cultural preferences and former consciences did not end with Christian conversion. Though all food is acceptable (I Timothy 4:4), a Jewish Christian had difficulty eating all meats. His past life had been regulated by a different divine law. As a result, spiritual tension developed between Jewish and Gentile Christians concerning proper food to eat. Regarding the problem, Paul stated that (1) they were not to pass judgment on each other; (2) they were not to cause anyone to stumble; (3) and they were not to use the right to eat meat to destroy a person for whom Jesus died (Romans 14). In Romans 14:16 Paul wrote, "Let not then your good be evil spoken of . . ." *What was right within itself was not to be used to produce an evil influence.* Being right or doing that which was right did not justify creating harmful influences. Doing what is right in a harmful manner can destroy other Christians. It was their responsibility to see such did not happen.

Jesus used two powerful illustrations to stress the responsibility of spiritual influence. In Matthew 5:13, He stated, "Ye are the salt of the earth; but if the salt have lost its savor, wherewith shall it be salted? It is thenceforth good for nothing, but to be cast out and trodden under foot of man." Because salt was the principal preservative of meat in Jesus' day, it was an impressive symbol of the power and outreach of influence. It was a highly taxed item. At times salt traders were taxed to the point of destroying their opportunity to make a profit. As a result traders often mixed other white crystalline salts with the sodium chloride. This increased the quantity of salt while decreasing the concentration of the sodium chloride. If the salt was "diluted" enough times as it passed from trader to trader, there would not be enough sodium chloride in the "salt" to preserve meat. Yet, even a small amount of sodium chloride would kill plant life. Worthless salt had to be thrown in the road to keep it from being harmful. Jesus' point is powerful. Christians are His spiritual salt. *However, Christians can dilute their lives with worldliness to the point that they have no useful spiritual influence.* At that point they become a destructive influence who produce only harm.

In Matthew 13:33 Jesus compared spiritual influence to leaven or yeast. A little yeast can make any amount of dough rise. It will work until the entire amount has been touched by its presence. *His disciples were to be His yeast in this world.* Christian influence was expected to work its way throughout society and the world.

## Selfishness — Influence's Enemy

*The ultra-selfishness which increasingly characterizes Americans should be of grave concern to all Christians.* The American society has been geared to everyone satisfying self. In almost everyone's life, "I" is the most important factor. The number one concern and top priority is "me." "Me" is the basic concern in every issue. Even beneficial social reforms are unlikely to occur because of people's overwhelming concern about how the change will affect "me." There is more concern for "me" than for the good of society.

The basic attitudes of society infiltrate the thinking of God's people. Theoretically, most Christians deplore selfishness. Practically, they find it convenient to become more selfish every year. A noticeable evidence of increasing Christian selfishness is seen in the popular attitude, "I am responsible for me, and only for me!" It generates this thinking: "My basic spiritual concern is me. You take care of yourself. If I know I am not sinning, nothing else matters. If I am misunderstood, that is not my problem." Too many Christians have forgotten that we are members of one another (Romans 12:5).

*Christians do not seem to realize that this concern with self, "my" desires, and "my" rights disclaims the responsibility of Christian influence.* It declares a Christian can belong to Christ while refusing to be His salt and yeast. It declares a Christian can follow a Lord who is interested in everyone while he is interested in no one. It affirms one can be a Christian and completely be disinterested in the influence his life exerts. These are deceitful, distorted, inaccurate concepts of the meaning of being a Christian.

Insofar as service and commitment to Christ, Christians never live for themselves. Every Christian is what he is because of the grace of God. He is physically and spiritually God-made. Christ died for Christians that they should no longer live for themselves but for Him who died for them (2 Corinthians 5:15).

## *Influence: A Debt To Others*

*In regard to Christian influence on sinners, the Christian never lives for himself.* Peter wrote in I Peter 2:11, 12:

> Beloved, I beseech you as sojourners and pilgrims, to abstain from fleshly lusts, which war against the soul; having your behavior seemly among the Gentiles; that, wherein they speak against you as evil doers, they may by your good works, which they behold, glorify God in the day of visitation.

This was written to persecuted Christians living under hard circumstances. They were not to forget they did not belong to this world. They were to behave in an uncondemnable fashion among the pagans. In time the power of their godly influence would demand respect.

In I Peter 2:15 Peter again wrote, "For so is the will of God, that by well-doing ye should put to silence the ignorance of foolish men." Christians will never out-argue the world. The world's criticisms and foolish arguments will never be silenced by out-talking the world. Christians disarm the ignorant and foolish by outliving them. Influence, not words, will disarm the enemies of the godly.

Further, Peter wrote in I Peter 3:15, 16:

> Sanctify in your hearts Christ as Lord: being ready always to give answer to every man that asketh you a reason concerning the hope that is in you, yet with meekness and fear; having a good conscience; that, wherein ye are spoken against, that they may be put to shame who revile your good manner of life in Christ.

Christ was to be set aside as *THE* Lord in their lives. The reality of their hope was to be so obvious that unbelievers would ask them how they maintained their hope. They were to answer as respectful gentlemen who lived in all good conscience. In this manner, those who reviled their good manner of life would be put to shame. Again, their enemies would not be defeated by arguments and words, but by the influence of an unconquerable, hopefilled life in Christ.

*In regard to Christian influence on Christians, the Christian never lives for himself.* Scripture gives continuing emphasis to the fact that Christians bear each other's burdens and seek each other's well-being (Galatians 6:1-5; Romans 15:1-3; Philippians 2:1-8). The heart of this responsibility rests in the reality that Christians are a family. Because Christians belong to Christ, they belong to each other. This spiritual family is sustained by *agape* love, the love which seeks the highest good of another. This is the love which moved Christ to die for all. As one Christian considers another, he must understand, "If my Lord died for you, and you are His child, I cannot hurt or discourage you by the way I live. Because He loves you, I must love you and be concerned about your well-being. His death made us family."

*The revival of a proper concern for Christian influence is urgently needed.* Concern about appropriate Christian dress, speech, pleasures, business practices, and associations must be renewed. That concern must not degenerate into Pharisaical laws and rules based on human judgments and evaluations. Rather, Christians must awaken to the fact that godly people look like, act like, and speak like godly people. When Christian people begin to look like, talk like, and act like the godless people around them, it is probable they have become like the godless people around them.

If a Christian has courage and faith, God can use him powerfully in any honorable walk of life. Being a powerful influence for Christ is basically a personal matter. Powerful spiritual influence is based primarily on what a person is within himself. Actions have great influence when they reflect the true person within. The only effective monitor of spiritual influence is a Christian's own clear, educated, honest conscience.

## *Questions*

1. What are some typical answers to the question, "How do I decide how I should act and speak?"
2. Illustrate the fact that the question of influence is commonly disregarded.
3. Discuss Romans 12:17. Who are "all men"?
4. What wise lessons concerning protecting Christian influence should be learned from 2 Corinthians 8:16–24?
5. What was the problem when Paul wrote, "Let not your good be evil spoken of . . ." (Romans 14:16)?
6. Why was salt a good symbol of influence (Matthew 5:13)? How could salt lose its savor? How can Christians lose their savor?
7. Discuss the problem of ultra-selfishness in society and in the church.
8. What are the basic inconsistencies of a Christian seeking to follow Christ and being interested only in "me"?
9. In regard to sinners, in what way must a Christian not live for himself? Discuss 1 Peter 2:11, 12; 2:15; 3:1; and 3:15, 16.
10. Explain this statement: in Christian-Christian relationships no Christian has the right to live for himself. Read some passages which support this statement.

## *Thought Questions*

1. In what ways can bad Christian influence hurt the church?
2. How does good Christian influence help the church?
3. What are some specific areas in which Christians need to be more concerned about their influence?
4. What is the most important lesson in this chapter?

# Chapter Seven

# A World Without Conscience

If a Christian stepped back two thousand years to Paul's world of the first century, he would find the experience distressing, traumatic, and deeply disturbing. Many Christians have romanticized the thought of stepping back to that world by imagining the excitement of experiencing the feel of the Apostles' world. Such an experience would prove far more terrifying than exciting. One cannot imagine what he would hear and see.

Many conditions of that age would deeply distress today's Christian. The slavery he encountered would shock and frighten him. In every major city slaves would outnumber free citizens. More disturbing than their number would be their identity. Indentured slaves included many former shopkeepers, businessmen, and farmers who could not pay their debts. Because bankruptcy did not exist, hard times and indebtedness could make anyone a slave. Among the slaves were the educated, the skilled, and the best trained people of nations other than Rome. They were the spoils of victory after a conquest. Many slaves came from the middle class and the elite of fallen societies.

Equally shocking and terrifying would be the attitude toward human life. An invitation to the circus was an invitation to entertainment unknown in this society. Commonly the entertainment was witnessing people in an arena fighting in a determined effort to kill each other. These death struggles included a battle between two gladiators, an "every man for himself" battle with many contestants, and pitched battles between two forces. Occasionally defenseless people would seek to flee from wild animals. Thousands would gather to cheer as they enjoyed the sport of violent human death.

Due to poverty, exposing infants was a common practice. Baby girls, considered a liability, often were taken outside of town shortly after birth and left to die of exposure. Some people made a livelihood by collecting and caring for abandoned infants until they could be sold as slaves. Human life was cheap.

The acceptance of and nature of sexual immorality would be distressing. Both male and female prostitution were more open, more common, and more accepted. Sacred prostitution was used to worship pagan goddesses by rites of fornication. Such temples maintained women to serve as sacred prostitutes. The temple of Aphrodite in Corinth had one thousand such women.

How does one account for such evil days and horrible conditions? Was it the result of savagery, primitive cultures, or substandard civilization? Was the world composed of ignorant, uneducated, unthinking people? History reveals those were not the reasons. Roman civilization still influences today's world. The great Greek culture was still alive and influential. The Jewish culture of that day directly influences Christianity of today. Writers, historians, artists, and philosophers of that period are still worthy of study.

How did that age become so insensitive and immoral? While no one factor produced those conditions, a major contributing factor was this: *they were a world without conscience.*

## *The Christian's Conscience*

In Scripture there is a strong emphasis on the importance of conscience. *sunadasis,* the Greek word translated conscience, means, "a knowing of oneself." It is the central self-consciousness of a knowing and acting person. Acknowledging a good and a bad and a right and a wrong, it is the awareness that personal conduct, intentions, and character must be measured by moral goodness.

Everyone has a conscience. While its values and standards are learned, the conscience itself is not acquired. Though it can be destroyed, everyone possesses one.

*The responsibility to develop and live by a godly conscience is taught clearly in Scripture.* Emphasis on the importance and the role of the conscience includes the following. Christians obey the laws of the land for conscience's sake (Romans 13:5). They accept the responsibility of not injuring the weaker conscience of unlearned Christians (I Corinthians 8:9–13). After learning to forsake false teachings, they learn to love out of a pure heart, a good conscience, and an unfeigned love (I Timothy 1:5). Holding to faith and a good conscience keeps them from shipwrecking the Christian faith (I Timothy 1:18, 19). Hopefilled Christians who cope with severe opposition ultimately win the respect of their revilers by holding to faith and a good conscience (I Peter 3:15, 16).

A Christian's responsibilities regarding the conscience include training it by the teachings and standards of the Word, living by it in all godliness, and respecting the consciences of other Christians. Considering social conditions in the first century, the instruction to educate and to live by one's conscience would have created a distinctively different life which others would not have understood. Today the difficulty and distinctiveness of living by conscience should be no surprise.

*A trained conscience is essential to Christian existence.* A trained conscience makes many evil, ungodly acts unthinkable. It makes one constantly aware of his responsibility for his own conduct and behavior. It increases one's sensitivity toward others and their lives. A godly, righteous life is impossible without a trained conscience.

## Conscience Blesses Society

*Citizens with strong, godly consciences are an invaluable asset to any society or nation.* The individual is the most effective regulator of human conduct in any society. A massive police force, stringent laws with severe penalties, or incentive rewards will never provide effective control of any society. People feeling the responsibility to control themselves is the most effective means of control in any society. Society benefits everytime a person accepts the moral responsibility to control himself. When many people accept that responsibility, the social benefit is broad based. A society with godly people of devout conscience in the majority reaps specific blessings. Homes are more stable. Children receive greater love and caring. Businesses are concerned about honesty and giving value. Laborers are more conscientious and more concerned about productivity. Crimes against people decline. Respect for law increases. Legislation will consider the best interest of all people.

That citizens of godly conscience are assets to a nation is not speculation. *The American society has demonstrated that truth.* Citizens who possessed strong consciences once characterized this nation. No longer ago than the 1950s, houses and outbuildings were left unlocked, tools were not locked away, and loaded cars were left unlocked. A missing tool or machine meant a neighbor had borrowed it. Business deals were made and honored with a promise and a handshake.

Earlier years were characterized by greater integrity. Communities would work and harvest a sick neighbor's crop or rebuild the house of a burned out family. Everyone knew each other and honored the unwritten law which declared that neighbors did not abuse neighbors. Strangers were welcomed and helped.

Those were not perfect times. While thieves and the dishonest existed, their conduct was regarded by most as unacceptable. Those without integrity were held in contempt, and their values did not rule the times.

Such conditions are unimaginable in today's society. Who has not had something stolen? How necessary are locks? Who trusts a stranger? Who regards the business world as basically honest? Who believes the American worker is conscientious and hard working? Almost everyone is skeptical, distrustful, and pessimistic about the honesty and integrity of most Americans.

No one would have believed any 1950 prophet who foretold the following would occur in America: (1) abortions would be used for birth control; (2) fornication would be practiced openly by middle and upper class Americans; (3) divorce and remarriage would be easy and commonplace; (4) drugs for pleasure would have popular endorsement; (5) white collar crime would be more costly than criminal theft; (6) homosexuality would be a legal lifestyle; and (7) private homes would need the protection of burglar alarms. Yet, more than this has come to pass.

Why? Is the American of today less educated? Does privation force people to act less civilized? Has cultural awareness and sophistication tumbled? Is it the result of an inferior lifestyle? Absolutely not! Americans on the whole are better educated with a higher standard of living, better developed culturally, more sophisticated, better informed, and have more control over their lifestyle than in any period of this nation's history. Then what has happened? Among the important changes is this one: too many Americans have become people without conscience. Concepts of right and wrong have drastically changed, and a growing number of people are convinced there is no right or wrong.

*How do people without consciences affect the American society?* Many can steal without guilt — office supplies, personal property, tax dollars, an employer's time. Many can abuse others without remorse — cheat them, lie to them, or physically harm them. Spouses can cheat on mates, children can be neglected or abused, and basic family needs can be ignored without concern. Corruption, bribery, graft, and fraud can exist in public offices and guilty officials be re-elected to their positions. The new creed is this: anything is acceptable if it is profitable or pleasurable.

## The Conscience Crisis

A reality more terrifying than those social conditions is the fact that too many Christians are becoming people without conscience. *The New Testament church is no longer the vanguard of the conscience.* There was a time when Christians would not attend any movie. Suitable music for entertainment was honestly discussed. A Christian woman would not publicly wear shorts. Christians would not swim in mixed groups. Christian men would not appear near nude in public. Virtually all Christians regarded dancing as anti-spiritual. Drinking was regarded inappropriate anywhere at anytime. Today many Christians engage in every one of these activities with no conscience problem.

Admittedly, those issues often were not approached Scripturally nor addressed wisely in those days. There was more concern for conformity than a clear understanding of Bible standards. Condemnations were too often based on personal preferences or prejudices which evaded real moral issues. Yet, most Christians used their conscience with definite standards of conduct to evaluate what they did. Sadly, that cannot be said of many Christians today.

*Activities and involvements contrary to Bible standards of holiness and purity trouble the conscience of too few Christians to-*

*day.* It is frightening to see how few object to using sexual lust for entertainment. Little thought is given to what one sees at the movies. Many Christian women sensually display their bodies without concern for the enticement they generate. Lewd lyrics of popular songs are enjoyed without concern for their influence or stimulation. Many Christians give little thought to how they find pleasure. Conscience is seldom an obstacle.

Integrity is sacrificed with equal ease. Too many Christians can lie, cheat, and be dishonest without guilt feelings. Many firmly believe that dishonesty is essential and necessary in the business world. Unethical practices are matter-of-fact realities, not matters of conscience. The Christian without conscience is too common.

What will become of the nation and the world if the Lord's church becomes a church without conscience? *If the American conscience is to be resurrected, Christians must be an unashamed people of conscience.* This society does not need a church who believes in Bible theories. God does not need a people who are experts in the theory of Bible principles. God needs knowledgeable children who have the courage and conviction to live by accurately trained consciences.

Christians have witnessed what people living without conscience have done to this nation. Will the same thing be permitted to happen to the Lord's church? The Lord's church will be a church with a conscience only when each individual Christian becomes a godly person of conscience.

## Questions

1. In what ways could a person become a slave in the first century?
2. Illustrate the fact that human life was cheap in the first century.
3. Discuss conditions concerning sexual morality in the first century.
4. What factor made a major contribution to creating such evil conditions?
5. What is a conscience? What does it do?
6. Use the following passages to discuss the importance of the conscience to a Christian:
   a. Romans 13:5
   b. 1 Corinthians 8:9–13
   c. 1 Timothy 1:5
   d. 1 Timothy 1:18, 19
   e. 1 Peter 3:15, 16
7. What are the Christian's basic responsibilities concerning the conscience?
8. Give some specific ways in which the conscience serves a Christian.

9. Why are godly consciences an invaluable asset to any society? Discuss the value of godly conscience to society.
10. From personal memories or family memories, illustrate the benefits of living in a community of people who honor the conscience.
11. Discuss some specific ways in which the absence of conscience has contributed to moral decay in this society.
12. Illustrate the fact that many Christians are becoming increasingly unconcerned about the conscience.

## *Thought Questions*

1. How does a Christian develop and mature his conscience?
2. What is the conscience of a congregation?
3. What are the benefits of being a part of a congregation who has a godly conscience?
4. What is the most important lesson in this chapter?

# Chapter Eight

# When the Cock Crows!

Satan does not command a one-battalion army equipped with a single gun of limited range. This capable enemy is equipped with an arsenal of weapons capable of waging deadly warfare against any state of spiritual existence. He can attack the spiritually strong as effectively and powerfully as he can the spiritually weak. Failure to realize that truth invites serious spiritual crisis or spiritual disaster.

Every Christian knows the spiritually enslaved sinner is controlled and manipulated by Satan. Being trapped by his own sin, rebellion, and weakness, the sinner is powerless to deliver himself. In every sense, he is Satan's victim.

The spiritually weak have reason to fear Satan because he will exploit effectively their weaknesses. With precise, effective temptations, he will seek to deceive them. Unless they build a strong relationship with God, they will become Satan's victims.

What about the spiritually strong? Is the person who has grown through his weakness, overcome temptation, built a knowledgeable faith, and committed himself to service and worship beyond Satan's attack?

Consider a paradox. Ask a Christian if he is spiritually strong, and he will affirm his spiritual weakness. Ask him if his weaknesses are serious enough to cause him to fall, and he will be offended. If his inner voice spoke it would say, "I may have my weaknesses, but I am much too strong to fall." The paradox is this: most Christians feel strong and weak at the same moment. They hold feelings of strength and of insecurity at the same time. Again the question arises: "Do the spiritually strong have reason to fear Satan? If so, what should they fear?"

## *Peter: An Exceptional Success*

Peter clearly illustrates the power of Satan to attack the spiritually strong. Peter deserves recognition as an exceptional person. *He was a decisive man — an admirable quality.* After working all night manually casting fishing nets from a boat (hard, sweat work!), he immediately accepted the invitation to follow Jesus. He did not say, "I am too tired to give your request proper thought and consideration." Or, "This is the wrong moment to make a decision that important." He made an immediate decision to give up his livelihood and to commit to a transient life of discipleship indefinitely.

*Peter was a wholehearted man.* He always knew his mind and heart. Circumstances never made him doubt his responsibilities nor his commitments. Not once in Jesus' ministry was Peter less than 100% for Jesus and 100% with Jesus.

*He was a perceptive man.* He had the exceptional, uncommon qualities of truly seeing and hearing. In John 6 when a multitude of disciples deserted Jesus because of a hard teaching, Jesus asked the Twelve if they were leaving. Peter replied, "Lord, to whom shall we go? Thou hast the words of eternal life" (John 6:68). Of the Twelve, only Peter perceived that Jesus was the Christ, the Son of the living God (Matthew 16:16). While this was a revelation, Peter was perceptive enough to make the revelation possible.

*Peter was a loyal man.* His loyalty made the idea of Jesus being killed unthinkable and unacceptable. If necessary he would die trying to prevent Jesus' death. No one was more openly, devoutly, and totally committed to Jesus.

Jesus recognized and paid tribute to these admirable qualities. Peter was one of Jesus' inner three disciples, no small honor. He was with Jesus on every special occasion. Jesus gave him the keys of the kingdom (Matthew 16:19). Peter opened the kingdom to the Jews in Acts 2 and to the Gentiles in Acts 10.

Though Peter always spoke out, he was not a braggard. Nor was he an arrogant man who loved to do grandstanding. What he said he felt; what he felt, he felt with his whole being. His thoughts were rooted in the convictions of his heart. Certainly he said too much on occasions, and at times his conviction lacked sound judgment. Often he was sure he was right because he was certain Peter could not be wrong. Because he overestimated his knowledge and understanding, he even had the confidence to tell Jesus He was wrong. Yet, none of this was arrogance; it was wholehearted commitment which exceeded accurate knowledge and sound judgment.

## *Peter: An Exceptional Failure*

Peter was a combination of notable successes and notable failures. His successes were many. He readily accepted discipleship and never looked back. He boldly stood by Jesus in the Garden of Gethsemane until Jesus made him put down the sword. After the ascension he was a courageous, masterful preacher. His courage in his arrests, trials, verbal defenses of Jesus, and abuse suffered deserves nothing but admiration.

Yet, Peter's failures were as notable as his successes. His denial of Jesus at the trials will never be forgotten. His complete disillusionment and return to his old occupation after the resurrection is always surprising.

Peter is a testimony to this truth: *committed Christians are commonly a combination of notable successes and notable failures.*

People who do great things for God are capable of making great mistakes. How can that be?

*The foundation of Peter's failures rested in Peter's faith.* Read Matthew 16:21-23. This incident happened shortly after Peter confessed Jesus to be the Christ. The One who Peter knew was God's Christ was saying the Jewish leaders were going to kill Him. Peter dogmatically contradicted Jesus' prediction by rebuking Jesus for that thought. Because he did not want that to happen, he would not let it happen.

Jesus who blessed Peter for his confession then called him Satan. Peter the confessor had become Peter the stumbling block. He had become a source of serious temptation to Jesus. The Greek root word for stumbling block means a bait stick for a trap. Peter was Satan's bait stick in a trap set for Jesus. Peter was appealing to Jesus' own desire not to die. Look at the contrast: in Matthew 16:16 the decisive Peter knew Jesus was the Christ; in 16:23 he was the bait stick in Satan's trap.

Read Matthew 26:31-35. Jesus said all the Twelve would be offended in Him that night and would flee like sheep when the shepherd is killed. Peter responded, "If all are offended, Lord, I will not be." Jesus replied, "You will deny me three times before the cock crows." Peter answered, "If it means dying with you, I will never deny you." All the disciples agreed they would not deny Jesus.

Mark 14:27-31 reveals the intensity of Peter's feelings in this incident. Verse 31 says Peter "exceedingly vehemently" declared he would not deny Jesus. The suggestion was so outrageous that he found it disgusting and unworthy.

Why did Peter so strongly deny the possiblity? *The weakness, the flaw in Peter's faith was this: Peter had enormous confidence, but his confidence was in Peter.* It was not his relationship with Jesus but his personal strength which was the source of his confidence. Peter trusted Peter's commitment, Peter's loyalty, Peter's judgment, and Peter's strength. Peter had such confidence in Peter that he could not imagine a trial bigger than Peter could handle. He believed in Jesus with all his being, but he placed his confidence in himself.

In spite of Peter's confidence in himself, he denied Jesus. Judas came with the soldiers and betrayed Jesus. Jesus was arrested and bound as though he were a dangerous criminal. Peter tried to prevent it. He fought the professional soldiers of the temple guard. He gladly would have died defending Jesus. However, he could not stand defenseless and die with Jesus. When Peter could not depend on Peter, his faith crumbled and his courage failed. Like the rest, he ran into the night. When the trials began, a timid, scared, bewildered Peter quietly came to the proceedings. Others recognizing him resulted in three denials of Jesus, the last with cursing and swearing.

The cock crowed, and Jesus looked at him. Crushed, shattered, disillusioned with himself, and inwardly devastated, Peter fled into the night weeping bitterly. No man ever cried with greater anguish, frustration, and despair. Wonder how Peter felt the three days preceding the resurrection?

## *Facing the Inevitable*

*This is an undeniable truth: every Christian who dares to grow and to mature in Christ will inevitably face a moment when the cock crows for him.* Satan's most powerful weapon against the spiritually strong is to attack their tendency to put confidence in themselves instead of in their relationship with the Lord. Today's Christian cannot be warned any more than Peter could be. While Christian self-confidence is essential for spiritual success, it is equally essential that faith not be founded in that self-confidence. Ironically, the stronger a Christian becomes, the more easily he believes he is taking care of the Lord rather than the Lord is taking care of him. Inevitably every growing Christian will be tested in ways he cannot imagine. As a result, he will find himself doing things he never imagined he would do. As certainly as this will happen to every Christian, that certainly will the cock crow for every Christian.

When the cock crowed for Peter, he wept, retreated, and was broken. Later, he let the Lord put him back together and make him a much stronger, more valuable servant. Today the question is not, "Will the cock crow at some point in my life for me?" It will. The real question is, "What will I do when the cock crows for me?" One can do many things. He can quit; become a permanent critic of the church; become a negative evaluator of all; never serve again; or be hurt, frustrated, and jealous. Or, he can let the Lord put his life back together, learn from the experience, and become a mightier servant.

*No one will trust the Lord instead of himself because he is told to do so.* That lesson must be learned through experience. Ironically, the Christian usually learns this lesson *after* he is convinced he is trusting the Lord. Had Peter been interviewed before entering the Garden of Gethsemane, and had he been asked if his faith was in Jesus or in Peter, he would have replied indignantly, "In Jesus, of course! Why do you think I follow Him, serve Him, and sacrifice for Him?" Yet, he actually believed in himself. Peter never knew that until the cock crowed.

There is a lot of Simon Peter in every strong Christian.

## Questions

1. What are the dangers of underestimating Satan's power as an enemy?
2. Discuss the common paradox which exists in most Christians concerning their personal spiritual strength.
3. Discuss the following admirable qualities in Peter's life:
   a. His decisiveness
   b. His wholeheartedness
   c. His perceptiveness
   d. His loyalty
   e. Which one of these is the most difficult to cultivate? Why?
4. Was Peter a thoughtless braggard? Explain your answer.
5. What were some of Peter's notable failures?
6. Read the following passages and discuss Peter's attitude and confidence.
   a. Matthew 16:21–23
   b. Matthew 26:31–35
   c. Mark 14:27–31 (especially verse 31)
7. Why did Peter strongly deny the possibility of his denying Jesus?
8. Demonstrate the fact that Peter tried to keep his promise to remain with Jesus to death.
9. What happened when Peter's confidence in himself proved insufficient?
10. Discuss the effect the sound of the crowing cock had on Peter. Why did it affect Peter this way?
11. What is Satan's most powerful weapon against the spiritually strong?
12. Illustrate the fact that Peter's notable failure did not destroy Peter spiritually.

## Thought Questions

1. Why is self-confidence essential to spiritual success?
2. When can self-confidence replace faith in the Lord? Does a Christian know this has happened to him?
3. What is the most important lesson in this chapter?

# Chapter Nine

# What Great Thing Can I Do For God?

Every Christian with a sensitive heart wants to do something great for God. Tenderhearted appreciation and deep-flowing affection for God and Christ produce a natural desire to do something great for God. This appreciation rises from many blessings: forgiveness received, release from guilt, the sense of peace with God, and the joy of knowing who one is and why one is living. Words are inadequate to express the depth of this appreciation. This burning, inexpressible sense of appreciation makes one yearn to do something special for God.

The desire to do a great thing for God is intensified by the seeming insignificance of what he is doing for God. Nothing he can do seems sufficiently important to show his gratitude. Nothing he does produces significant changes or benefits for God. He is powerless to change the world, society, or even his own community. All he does seems to be so little for so much received.

The desire to do something great for God is both good and dangerous. In many ways it is a good desire. There is spiritual benefit in being sensitive to the Lord's love and care, in knowing one's blessings, and in feeling the debt of gratitude. Such sensitivity generates a natural love for God and creates willing responsiveness to God. The finest motives for service and obedience are produced by such sensitivity.

To realize one's indebtedness to the Lord is a blessing. Proper attitudes and feelings for the Lord are more easily produced when one is aware of his indebtedness. The knowledge of undeserved blessings is effective protection against arrogance, pride, and stubborness. Christians with this heart are rarely hostile toward or resentful of God.

The desire to do something great can result in a life of Christian service. Christians involved in the Lord's work on a continuing basis are self-motivated, steadfast, and dependable. They have an obvious, deep appreciation for Christ. They do not serve because they have to but because they want to serve.

The desire to do something great for the Lord can also be dangerous. One can feel anything he can do is insignificant, unimportant, and worthless to God. He can feel incapable of doing anything genuinely meaningful. Because he wants to do something great but is convinced he cannot, he can easily become a defeatist who possesses a terrible spiritual self-image.

## Defining A "Great Thing"

Most Christians are certain they never have done anything great for God. If asked if have they done something great, most might reply, "I have never given Him an expensive gift. I have never been an elder, preacher, or missionary. Nothing significant in the world has changed because of me. No, I have done nothing which could be classified as great."

*What properly can be classified as a "great thing"?* What makes an act or deed a "great thing"? How are "great things" distinguished from "insignificant things"? Is it a matter of results? Is it the magnitude of the deed? Is it the impact the deed has on society? Is it measured in continuing influence? Is it determined by the number of people affected? Is it a matter of the changes which result from the deed?

In the New Testament, who did great things for Christ? If Christians made a list, almost everyone would include Paul, Peter, John, Barnabas, Timothy, and Titus. Most lists would be surprisingly short.

*Christians need to be certain they properly define a "great thing."* Make a list of those who did "great things" for Jesus. The list definitely would include the Apostles. While they would be a unanimous choice, virtually nothing is known about the lives and deeds of most of the Apostles. Apollos, the eloquent preacher, would be on the list. However, not one sermon of this dynamic preacher is preserved. Luke, the author of a gospel and Acts and a missionary companion of Paul's, would be on the list. Yet, little is known about what he did and where he served. So many names associated with greatness are of Christians about whom little is known.

## Examples of Greatness

In contrast, consider people Jesus called great. In Matthew 8:5–13 Jesus met *a Roman centurion* whose name is unknown. He came to beg Jesus to heal a sick, suffering servant. When Jesus agreed to go with him to the servant, the officer begged Jesus not to come to his house because he felt unworthy for Jesus to enter his home. If Jesus would merely speak the word, he knew his servant would be healed. Jesus said, "I have not found so great faith, no not in Israel." While his name is unknown, the greatness of his faith has lived for almost two thousand years. All he did was express complete confidence in the full power and authority of Jesus.

In Matthew 15:21–28 *a Canaanitish woman* begged Jesus to heal her daughter. He refused to hear her pleas. Finally, because her pleas disturbed the disciples, they begged Jesus to send her away.

He declared a hard, stern fact: he was sent only to the lost of Israel. When the woman continued reverencing him and pleading, Jesus told her bluntly it was not proper to give the children's bread to the dogs. She replied, "Even the dogs eat of the crumbs which fall from the master's table." Jesus then responded, "O woman, great is thy faith: be it done unto thee even as thou wilt." Except for this incident, the woman is unknown. Yet, the greatness of her faith is known two thousand years later.

In Mark 12:41–44 Jesus watched those making contributions to the temple treasury. Some of the rich gave large, impressive sums. *A widow* passed by and gave two mites, approximately a penny. While Jesus made no comment about the gifts of the rich, he said this widow gave more than all the rest. They gave of their profits; she gave her whole living. Not one name of the rich contributors is known, nor the amount he gave. Every child in Bible class knows the widow who gave a penny. The widow who gave a penny taught the unforgettable lesson on giving and generosity, not the wealthy contributors. In Jesus' eyes, what the widow did was truly great.

Many did small things which were great in God's eyes. Most Christians know *Dorcas* (Acts 9:36–43). She was so loved and appreciated that upon her death friends hurriedly walked from Joppa to Lydda to beg Peter to come. Who was this woman? What did she do to cause others to seek earnestly her resurrection? She made clothes for the widows of her community.

*Onesimus* is the central figure of the small book of Philemon. What great thing did he do to cause an Apostle to write a letter in his behalf, a letter which is Scripture? He was a runaway slave who fled to Rome. He happened to find the imprisoned Paul, his Christian master's friend. He cared for Paul's physical needs and was converted to Christ. Paul so appreciated Onesimus' service that he sent Onesimus back to Philemon declaring he was to be received as a Christian brother. His great thing was his service to Paul.

By most people's standards, Dorcas and Onesimus did nothing significant, earthshaking, nor of lasting importance. By God's standards, their deeds were of such significance that their names will never die.

Consider the memorable characters of Jesus' parables. Who are the inspiring, heart-touching characters who created unforgettable impressions? Were they kings or people of noble birth, of wealth, and of power? The unforgettable characters are *a shepherd* who searched for one lost sheep, *a prodigal son* who returned home, *a Samaritan* who helped an injured Jew, and *a widow* who pled with an unrighteous judge.

## God's Definition

Obviously, the Lord's definition of a great thing and people's common definition of a great thing are in distinct contrast. *With the Lord, anyone, regardless of economic condition or social status, is capable of doing a great thing.* Every Christian needs to understand that any Christian can do something great for God. Any Christian can do great things which urgently need to be done.

By God's definition living *a consistent, godly life* is a great thing. Controlling the mind, the tongue, and the body and using each for righteousness is greatness. Few Christians present God this gift.

Being a person of *compassion* is a great thing. Helping people instead of condemning them is a rare quality of greatness. Feeling for people rather than being disgusted with them was a quality of Jesus' greatness.

*Trusting God* with one's life and future is a great thing. Having the faith to live today fully and to trust God with tomorrow is greatness. Trusting God's promises with full confidence is greatness. Serving the Lord with assurance rather than wasting life in worry is greatness. These are uncommon qualities of greatness.

*Forgiveness* is a great thing. It is greatness to refuse grudges, bitterness, and hostility a place in the heart, or to possess a love which hurt cannot overshadow. To use forgiveness to build a future with those who have been offensive is greatness measured by Jesus' example and image.

The list of great things is almost endless: *mercy, kindness, unselfish service,* and *steadfastness* with all their kindred feelings, attitudes, and acts. If one doubts the greatness of these qualities, do two things: note the value God and Christ place on each of them in the New Testament; note how few people become a person possessing those qualities.

Jesus declared those faithful in little would be faithful in much (Luke 16:10). Doing God's great things prepares a person to do the things Christians consider great. *Great servants of God are built through years of doing small things of true greatness.*

Imagine all the happenings in the early church people would thrill to know. What was Peter's most spectacular miracle? What was Paul's largest audience? What was Apollos' greatest sermon? What congregation had the greatest number of baptisms? What were the most phenomenal deeds of the Apostles? All such questions are fascinating but unanswerable.

With all the fascinating material to write about, the Holy Spirit preserved the deeds of nameless people who did far less to change the world than any Apostle: a centurion who wanted a servant healed, a Gentile woman begging for her daughter's health, and a widow who gave a penny. The names of a woman who clothed widows and a runaway slave were preserved. Stories about a rebellious son who left home, a despised Samaritan who helped a Jew, and a widow who worried a judge were preserved. Why were these things preserved for future generations? In God's eyes, these represented a greatness He did not want forgotten, a greatness to be preserved until the end of time. This is the greatness within the capability of all.

Do something great for God. Be a devout, committed Christian. Live for the Lord daily. Fulfill each day's opportunities without considering how big or little the deeds are. Years of such living will result in true greatness by God's definition.

## Questions

1. Why do sensitive-hearted Christians want to do something great for God?
2. Why is it a blessing for a person to realize his indebtedness to God?
3. Illustrate the fact that the desire to do something great for God is the springboard for a life of Christian service.
4. How can the desire to do something great for God be dangerous?
5. Why is it difficult to distinguish between a "great thing" and an "insignificant thing"?
6. How much is known about people such as the Apostles who did great things?
7. Name three people Jesus said did something great and tell what each did.
8. What is noteworthy about Dorcas and Onesimus? What lesson about greatness is to be learned from them?
9. Who are the most memorable characters in Jesus' parables? Discuss what each did.
10. Explain this statement: God's definition of a great thing and people's common definition of a great thing are in distinct contrast.
11. Discuss some great things all people are capable of giving God.
12. If a person wants to do something great for God, how should he begin?

## Thought Questions

1. What is God's definition of a great thing?
2. Why is there so much difference between God's definition and people's definition?
3. What advice would you give a person who wants to do something great for God?
4. What is the most important lesson in this chapter?

# Chapter Ten

# Life's Two Bank Accounts

The desire to be rewarded for one's labors and efforts is a proper expectation. Scripture declares that a person's right to benefit from his labors is a basic right of man. This right exists in regard to physical and spiritual labors.

Receiving rewards and benefits for physical labor has always been acknowledged by God as a rightful expectation. The law of Moses declared that the ox which treaded out grain was not to be muzzled (Deuteronomy 25:4). A common method for threshing ripe wheat and barley used an ox and a threshing floor. The ox which was tied to a pivoting pole walked in a continuous circle. Shocks of ripened grain were thrown in its path. The grain fell from the stalks as the ox walked on them. The law of Moses declared that the ox which did the work had a right to eat of the shocks. Paul referring to this same law said it was written to declare that *every man had the right to benefit from his labors* (I Corinthians 9:9, 10). Referring to the law again, Paul wrote, "The laborer is worthy of his hire" (I Timothy 5:18).

Those who serve the Lord as a livelihood have the same rightful expectation. The Old and New Testaments plainly teach *those who use their lives in the work of the Lord have the right to be supported from their work.* The priests were the primary laborers for the Lord among the Jews. The temple sacrifices constituted a large part of their livelihood. Aaron and his sons received the meal offering for food (Leviticus 6:16). The priest who offered the sin offering was to be given the meat for food (Leviticus 6:26). The priests and their sons ate the meat of the trespass offerings (Leviticus 7:6). The meat from the peace offerings and all heave-offerings belonged to the priests (Leviticus 7:32; Numbers 5:9). Other sacrifices which became the priests' property included these: wave offerings, the best of the oil, the best of the wine, the best of the grain and all first fruit offerings, and all first-born animals given to God (Numbers 18:8–20). This was the reason for these becoming the priests' property: "It is your reward in return for your service in the tent of meeting" (Numbers 18:31).

Paul, referring to this provision in the Mosaical system, declared, "Even so did the Lord ordain that they that proclaim the gospel should live of the gospel" (I Corinthians 9:14). Jesus forbade the disciples to carry any provisions when he sent them on the limited commission because, "The laborer is worthy of his food" (Matthew 10:10).

In the same manner, *Christians have the right to be rewarded for their service to Christ.* The anticipation of reward is not the sole reason for rendering spiritual service. Love for Christ, the appreciation of forgiveness, and gratitude for salvation are powerful reasons for serving. However, expectation of reward is an important motivation. The author of Hebrews stated that God's great people of the Old Testament made their sacrifices because they sought a better, heavenly country (Hebrews 11:15, 16). Jesus endured the shameful disgrace of the cross because of the joy set before Him (Hebrews 12:2). In every age God has rewarded His people.

There are two spiritual avenues through which God rewards His people. There are two realms of reward promised to those who serve the Lord. Those two realms of rewarding are material blessings and treasures in heaven.

## Material Rewards

Consider the area of material blessings. *Christians are promised material blessings.* Peter quoting from Psalms 34:12 wrote, "For he that would love life, and see good days, let him refrain his tongue from evil, and his lips that they speak no guile . . . " (I Peter 3:10). Jesus said, ". . . Give, and it shall be given unto you; good measure, pressed down, shaken together, running over, shall they give into your bosom. For with what measure ye mete it shall it be measured to you again" (Luke 6:38). Discussing the difficulty of the rich being saved, Jesus said, "And everyone that hath left houses, or brethren, or sisters, or father, or mother, or children, or lands, for my name's sake, shall receive a hundredfold, and shall inherit eternal life" (Matthew 19:29). Jesus' best known statement concerning material blessings is this: "Seek ye first his kingdom and his righteousness, and all these things shall be added unto you" (Matthew 6:33).

These statements are not the promise of unlimited wealth or the promise of having everything one desires. Basically it is the promise that the material blessings a Christian receives will exceed the sacrifices he makes for Christ. However, one must be careful not to isolate these promises from Jesus' other declarations. Jesus often predicted that His disciples would face and endure sufferings, persecutions, sacrifices, rejection, and hatred.

*The promise of material blessings is both definite and conditional.* Society's acceptance of or rejection of Christians affects the extent they can be blessed materially. The extent of material prosperity is affected greatly by the age; times of persecution will not allow the prosperity of times of tolerance. Periods of material gain and material loss existed in the first-century church. Christians enjoyed material blessings produced by generous believers in the early Jerusalem church (Acts 2:44, 45). Many of those Christians likely lost everything when they fled the Jerusalem persecution (Acts 8:1-3). Evidence indicates that Christians at Corinth and Philippi were prosperous. Unquestionably, the church at Laodicea was prosperous. Yet, the Christians addressed in I Peter lived under different circumstances. Those to whom Hebrews 10:32-34 was written had suffered great material losses.

Though circumstances affect the extent of the blessings, God's people will receive material blessings. Those who serve and sacrifice for His glory can expect material rewards. In no age have Christians been blessed materially more richly than in this generation.

## Heavenly Rewards

Consider treasures in heaven. *Deeds done and sacrifices made for the Lord become treasures in heaven.* Christians are assured that not one deed, not one sacrifice is pointless or made for nought. Sacrificial decisions made for the Lord shall be rewarded beyond imagination or measure. The certainty of heavenly rewards assures the Christian that no sacrifice, regardless of its nature or size, is ever meaningless or a loss.

Jesus referred to treasures in heaven a number of times. When the rich young man inquired of Jesus how to receive eternal life, Jesus declared he would have treasures in heaven if he sold his possessions, gave to the poor, and followed Him (Matthew 19:21). Jesus told a group,

> Sell that which ye have, and give alms; make for yourselves purses which wax not old, a treasure in the heavens that faileth not, where no thief draweth near, neither doth moth destroyeth (Luke 12:33).

Jesus' best known statement was made in the Sermon on the Mount:

> Lay not up for yourselves treasures upon the earth, where moth and rust consume, and where thieves break through and steal: but lay up for yourselves treasures in heaven, where neither moth nor rust consume, and where thieves do not break through nor steal: for where thy treasure is, there will thy heart be also (Matthew 6:19-21).

## The Problem

These two reservoirs of reward pose a practical, everyday problem for every Christian. *First, it is extremely difficult not to prefer overwhelmingly the material rewards.* While all confess theoretically their preference should be the eternal rewards, most Christians also confess that material rewards tend to be their actual preference. It is a unique Christian who does not fight a daily war attempting to keep the reality of heavenly treasures equal to the realities of material rewards. When facing an actual, sacrificial choice between heavenly treasure and immediate material benefit, he often finds the promise of heavenly treasures to be no more than a hollow sound.

*Second, keeping one's thinking straight on a day-to-day basis is extremely difficult.* The basis of the problem is not the evil of possessing. Material things are not evil, and possessing is not evil. There is no virtue in poverty for poverty's sake. The problem lies in one's obsession with possessions and with possessing. The evil exists in one's attitude toward possessions and in the power possessions have in his life. Evil exists in the attitudes of coveteousness, lust for things, greed, envy, and jealousy. These attitudes form one of the most specific evils of life. They are among the most common evils in Christians today.

The problem is intensified by a lack of faith in the reality of heavenly treasures. Christians chide the rich young man for loving his possessions and shake their heads at the rich man who thought only of bigger barns and personal ease. Were they in similar situations, the majority would think exactly as the young man and rich farmer thought. Every Christian should understand the rich young man's problem. When he looked at his actual possessions and considered unseen heavenly treasures, he did not have faith enough to make heaven's treasures as real as his possessions. This inability to trust the reality of heavenly treasures plagues every Christian. Though the Lord promised them, in the privacy of one's mind heavenly treasures seem imaginary, indefinable, or highly questionable.

*Third, Christians have the wrong attitude toward heavenly treasures.* An as illustration, consider Christians who are examining a spiritual work which needs to be done but holds little promise of success. They commonly decide, "It would be a waste of time, accomplish nothing, and give us nothing to show for the effort." To know how many works clearly desired by God are rejected because Christians feel that they would be a profitless waste of time would be frightening. The beauty of treasures in heaven must be seen. When one does what Jesus wants done, regardless of the results, it is never a waste of time. It is impossible to receive nothing for any work which the Savior wishes done. Doing the works of the Lord generates treasures in heaven. Those treasures depend only on doing the Savior's wishes with the proper mind and heart.

When Christians are taken advantage of as they serve the Lord, some will say, "Do something nice for people and see what happens! Act like the Lord wants, and people use you! I will never learn! I was taken again!" When one is abused as he serves the Lord, his viewing the situation as "having been taken" is destructive to his heart and faith. When "being taken" finally results in bitterness and resentment, he will cease acting as the Lord wants.

Again, the beauty of treasures in heaven must be seen. If his attitude and heart are right, a Christian never loses as much as he gains when someone takes advantage of his godliness. When his godliness is unaffected by the abuse of his kindness, he increases the Lord's approval of his life. People may abuse him, but the Lord rewards him. People abused Jesus' kindness to the point of crucifixion, but God made Him King of kings and Lord of lords.

Sadly, a Christian's own spiritual family often opposes him as he seeks to be compassionate and serving. Many will say to him, "You are too kind to people! You let them take advantage of you! Get wise and be realistic!" This attitude is built on the belief that a Christian is a loser if people take advantage of his kindness. Treasures in heaven declare that nothing could be further from the truth. If he will be the finest Christian that he is capable of being, he is a winner regardless of the abuse he receives. *The God whose eye is upon the sparrow will see even the smallest kindness, and that kindness becomes treasure in heaven.* Treasures in heaven make it impossible to be too nice or too kind.

## Acknowledging The Reality

How does one deposit treasures in heaven? Read 1 Timothy 6:17-19 and note Paul's simple explanation. Doing good, being rich in good works, and being generous builds treasures in heaven. According to the parable of the judgment, giving food to the hungry, giving water to the thirsty, aiding the stranger, clothing the naked, and visiting the sick and imprisoned become treasures in heaven (Matthew 25:31-46). It is life's simplest bank account in which to make a deposit.

The writer of Hebrews said, ". . . He that cometh to God must believe that he is, and that he is a rewarder of them that seek after him" (Hebrews 11:6b). That is a sobering declaration. One cannot come to God unless he believes in God's ability to reward those who seek Him. Confidence in God's ability to reward is an essential part of acceptable faith.

A Christian consciously should carry two mental bank accounts. When he is prone to feel sorry for himself, to feel financially stressed, and to wonder how he will manage his material needs and commitments, he should examine his mental bankbook of God's material blessings. He should force himself to take time to think about the specific material blessings of his life. He will be amazed, ashamed, and unbelieving of all he has received. It will not end the war, but it will restore a proper perspective.

When his helpfulness produces no perceivable results, when his godly attitudes are abused, when his kindness is rebuffed with criticism, or when his labors produce little, he should examine his mental heavenly treasures bankbook. He examines this account *only* to remind himself he has made another deposit. He wants to be unable to forget that godly deeds are never wasted. He never, never wants to forget the reality of heavenly treasures.

## Questions

1. Deuteronomy 25:4 is the commandment not to muzzle the ox which treads out the grain.
   a. Explain the original commandment.
   b. What did Paul teach concerning this law in 1 Corinthians 9:9, 10?
   c. What did Paul say in 1 Timothy 5:18?
   d. What basic principle does all this teach?
2. List the benefits the Jewish priests received in the Old Testament. Why were they given these benefits (Numbers 18:31)?
3. What does 1 Corinthians 9:14 teach concerning those who proclaim the gospel?
4. Does this same principle apply to all Christians? Explain your answer.
5. What two specific realms of spiritual blessings exist for Christians?
6. What promises are made or implied in the following passages:
   a. 1 Peter 3:10
   b. Matthew 19:29
   c. Matthew 6:33
7. How are the promises of material blessings conditional? Illustrate your answer.
8. What are treasures in heaven? What assurance do they give?
9. Discuss the following references concerning treasures in heaven:
   a. Matthew 19:21
   b. Luke 12:33
   c. Matthew 6:19–21
10. In regard to preferring material blessings, what is *not* the basis of the problem? What *is* the basis of the problem?
11. Carefully explain the following statements:
    a. Because of treasures in heaven, one cannot "waste his time" by doing God's will.
    b. If someone takes advantage of a Christian, the Christian gains more than he loses because of treasures in heaven.
    c. Because of treasures in heaven, a Christian cannot be too nice or too kind.
12. How are deposits made into heavenly treasures?

## *Thought Questions*

1.  How can a Christian increase his desire for and preference for treasures in heaven?
2.  Why is the battle between the desire for material blessings and the desire for spiritual blessings a constant, everyday struggle?
3.  How can a Christian use the awareness of material blessings to strengthen himself spiritually?
4.  What is the most important lesson in this chapter?

# Chapter Eleven

# God's Power to Utilize People

When only the tasks of world evangelism, of edifying existing congregations, and of Christian benevolence are considered, the amount of work to be done for God is incomprehensible. When only one community is examined in regard to opportunities for compassion for the sick and elderly, for edifying the weak, for encouraging the troubled, for teaching the young, for reaching the distressed, and for doing good works, the task seems overwhelming. If the spiritual needs of one community are multiplied by all communities on earth, it is obvious that God needs an enormous work force. There is no talent or ability He does not need. His work is so diversified He can utilize anyone.

Suppose God composed a complete list of specific "jobs to be done" in today's world. Suppose every Christian had to examine that list carefully and select tasks he or she felt capable of doing. How many Christians would feel capable of doing nothing? If God had the freedom to use you in any way He wished, what could he accomplish through your life? How many Christians believe, "God could accomplish nothing significant through me. I have too little ability to be worth much to God. If God wants something important done, He will have to use someone else."

There are many tragic beliefs about God's ability to use people for His purposes. First, Christians commonly believe God cannot use "common people" to do anything important. Second, they believe He must use an extraordinary person if He is going to do something powerful, to cause a momentous change, or to cause an extraordinary happening. Third, they believe such individuals are rare with only a few living in each generation. Since most Christians believe themselves to be limited-ability persons, they are convinced God can make little use of them. Thus they sit waiting for God to find an exceptional person to do His work. As a result, many of God's important works go undone.

Most Christians find it difficult to discuss what they believe God can do with their individual lives. Some feel such discussion is presumptuous and arrogant. Others fear they will find previously unassumed responsibilities. Many feel so worthless that they regard such discussions as pointless. Most beliefs about God's ability to use people are in grave error. Jesus readily illustrates that error.

## The Impressive Jesus

Jesus was undeniably impressive in many ways. *His accomplishments are impressive.* Regardless of who evaluates Jesus' life, no one can deny His life changed the course of world history. His life, teachings, and death produced changes in social structures, human values, ethical teachings, and moral standards unparalleled by any other person. The impact of His life has been a major world influence for almost two thousand years. The world will not outgrow the impact of the Man from Galilee because His influence is woven into the fabric of many of the world's societies. While Jesus' influence on everything from literature to social consciousness could be discussed at length, suffice it to say that the impact of Jesus' life, teachings, and death is impressive.

*What Jesus was as a man is impressive.* Those who possess sensitivity and feeling for people are powerfully attracted to the man Jesus through the gospels. The phenomenal qualities of His life grip them. (1) He touches them with His concern for unwanted, unimportant people: a leper; a widow who lost an only son; a prostitute; a despised tax collector; the maimed. (2) He touches them by treating every person as an individual. Society's prejudicial stereotyping never influenced the way Jesus treated anyone. (3) He touches them with a compassion so great that it felt for those who tried to exploit Him, and it asked for forgiveness for those who killed Him in ignorance. (4) He touches them with a commitment to God's will which could not be swayed by the emotions of His disciples or the pressures of powerful enemies. (5) He touches them with the forcefulness of His teachings.

The man He was made what He said powerful. Had it not been for His unique life, His message may have been striking and curious, but not powerful and life changing. The trustworthiness and power of His message are founded in the life he lived and death he died. In all this, Jesus was most impressive.

## The Unimpressive Jesus

From another perspective, Jesus was not impressive. *His life situation and life circumstances were most unimpressive.* He was born in a small, insignificant village whose only claim to fame was some notable former residents. Part of His infancy was spent in exile in Egypt. He grew up in Nazareth, and insignificant town not even mentioned in the Old Testament. The man who served as His earthly father was a carpenter — not a priest, a Levite, a prophet, or a Jewish aristocrat. All Jesus' credentials for His mission and work were wrong. He was not trained in the schools of the Holy City, He never sat at the feet of a prominent rabbi, and He never lived in Jerusalem's prestigious spiritual environment. He grew up in, lived in, and died in poverty. He owned nothing but the clothes

He wore. Prominent religious leaders of His day did not arise from that background.

*Jesus left no descendants.* No sons perpetuated His name and legacy. As an adult He did not travel outside the tiny nation of Israel. No powerful, popular figure was His confidant or friend. No influential person openly championed His cause.

*Capernaum* served as the Galilean base for His ministry. This rural community was noted for business and commerce, not for religious influence. *His disciples* were untrained in communicating with and teaching people and had no preparation for beginning a religious movement. Among them were some fishermen, a tax collector, a radical Zealot, and others of unknown backgrounds. As far as is known, all had rural backgrounds with no education under a recognized Jewish rabbi.

*The Jewish religious communities never accepted Him.* Religious leaders resented Him as a public embarrassment and a threat to the nation's future. They ceaselessly opposed Him.

Today no one would seek to produce the world's Savior by using a man of Jesus' background and life situation. His background and life's circumstances were completely wrong for His mission and His purpose. Yet, He succeeded. He succeeded so powerfully that the world cannot destroy His influence or ignore the reality of His accomplishment. God powerfully used Jesus to succeed in a manner that defies human planning.

## Jesus: Not An Exception

Looking at God's achievement through Jesus' unimpressive life circumstances, most would say, "That is remarkable — even astounding. However, He was God's Son, and that makes Him unique." Being God's Son made Jesus unique. However, what God did with Jesus is not unique. It has been commonplace for God to use people of unimpressive credentials to achieve His purposes.

There was nothing impressive about Noah's life circumstances. Abraham was a nomad who wandered around the area of Palestine and Egypt as a man without a country. Joseph was betrayed by his brothers, lived as a slave, and lived as a powerless, forgotten prisoner. As a shepherd in rugged Judea, David spent little time with people; that is hardly impressive training to be a king. Daniel was a captive, a hostage, and a prisoner of war. Esther was an orphan of exiled Jewish parents. Nehemiah was a descendant of captive people, a victim of the Babylonian captivity, and a royal slave who served the king his wine. Ezekiel was a priest with no temple who was a captive in a foreign land. Amos was a herdsman. Matthew was a tax collector. Peter, Andrew, James, and John were fishermen.

God used few people of illustrious background to accomplish

His purposes. The only three prominent figures of illustrious backgrounds are Moses, Luke, and Paul.

There is a needed lesson to be seen in God's use of people of unimpressive backgrounds. *God has tremendous power to use anyone regardless of who he is or where he is.* God wants and can use anyone regardless of his background or his circumstances. The question is never "if" God can use a person. In God's countless tasks to be done, He can use everyone to do something. The question is not, "Can God use a person?" The question is, "Will the person allow God to use him?" The difference between Noah, Abraham, Esther, Nehemiah, and Peter and the thousands who did not serve God was not some exceptional ability which set them apart as extraordinary people. The difference was found in the trust each of them placed in God. Their courage to allow God to use them was the difference.

## The Proper Focus

Many Christians fail to allow God to use them because their spiritual focus is wrong. Being faithul is the common concern of all Christians. In their anxiety about faithfulness, many Christians try to define faithfulness to the nearest half-an-ounce or thirty-second of an inch. While no one wants to oppose proper concern for faithfulness, *Christians need to realize they are pursuing faithfulness in the wrong way.* One does not worry his way to faithfulness or define his way to faithfulness. When Christians have the faith and courage to let God use them freely, they are faithful. Knowledgeably doing God's will and work is faithfulness.

Following are some questions every Christian should ask himself. "What do I plan to accomplish for God? What are my spiritual dreams for serving Christ? Is what I am doing now all I ever plan to do? Am I at my spiritual peak rendering the best God can ever expect of me? Or am I growing? Will my growth allow God greater future use of my life? Do I live with a sense of spiritual mission knowing God's works are of eternal importance?"

The Christian who believes God uses only unique people of exceptional ability must realize that belief is a lie, a deceit from Satan. Most people who accomplish God's great tasks were unusual only in their faith and courage. Faith and courage are developed, not endowed.

God has urgent need for countless workers. The Christian who renders little or no service to God needs to ask himself, "Why has God been unable to make greater use of my life?" The answer to that question is the doorway to greater service.

## Questions

1. State two tragic beliefs among Christians concerning God's ability to use people.

2.  What is the effect of these tragic beliefs?
3.  Why do Christians find it difficult to discuss what they believe God can accomplish through them?
4.  Discuss the fact that Jesus' life was impressive in terms of what He accomplished.
5.  Discuss the unimpressive things about Jesus the man.
6.  Why do Christians often disregard the example of Jesus as proof that God can use anyone powerfully?
7.  How do the following people illustrate God's ability to utilize people?

    a. Noah            f. Esther
    b. Abraham         g. Nehemiah
    c. Joseph          h. Matthew
    d. David           i. Peter, Andrew, James, and John
    e. Daniel          j. Can you suggest other examples?

8.  What was the difference between the people of question 7 and those who did not serve God?
9.  What will not produce faithfulness?
10. How is faithfulness produced?

## Thought Questions

1.  Why must all Christians have full confidence in God's ability to use them?
2.  How will a Christian be affected by the belief that God cannot use him?
3.  How can a Christian produce a growing, continuing confidence in God's ability to use him?
4.  In regard to God's ability to use anyone, what lessons should be learned from Jesus? Be specific.
5.  What is the most important lesson to be learned in this chapter?

# Chapter Twelve

# Beautiful In the Eyes of God

Define the words "beautiful" and "ugly." What qualities distinguish "beautiful" from "ugly"? Distinguishing between beauty and ugliness is difficult. While anyone can define the two for himself, few can define successfully what is beautiful and ugly to everyone else.

Definitions of beauty and ugliness are highly individualistic. What is beautiful to one person is often ugly to another, and vice versa. If something is regarded as beautiful by a person, it must fulfill his definition and concept of beauty. Regardless of other's opinions, it is ugly if it does not fit his concept of beauty.

The fact that beauty is an individual concept is understood clearly by all. However, many have not understood that God's concept of beauty also is His own. No person defines for God His concept of beauty. If a person is beautiful to God, he fits God's concept of beauty.

## God's Definition

God does not define beauty by using the criteria people commonly use. *God never uses physical, outward appearance to determine beauty.* When the prophet Samuel examined Jesse's sons in search of the next king of Israel, he was much impressed with Eliab's appearance. God declared to Samuel, "Look not at his countenance, or on the height of his stature; because I have rejected him: for God seeth not as man seeth; for man looketh on the outward appearance, but Jehovah looketh on the heart" (I Samuel 16:7). Nothing in a person's outward appearance impresses God. God looks upon the inner beauty of the heart.

*God never uses the origin or culture of a person as a criteria of beauty.* People of one culture seldom see beauty in people of another distinctively different culture. People of Oriental cultures rarely describe "round-eyed" Caucasians as beautiful. People of African cultures would not consider the American Indian or Eskimo as beautiful. Cultural preferences and prejudices strongly influence definitions of beauty.

The Jewish people of the New Testament illustrate this fact. Their descent from Abraham was a source of great pride. They had little appreciation for other peoples, and they had no appreciation for the Samaritans. Under no circumstances would a Samaritan be beautiful to a Jew. Samaritans were dogs unfit for Jewish association.

This cultural prejudice blinded the Apostles to Jesus' desire to preach the gospel to all peoples. Only a divine revelation could convince Peter to enter a Gentile's house and preach the gospel to him (Acts 10). It took an angel to get Peter the Jew and Cornelius the Gentile together. Only a divine sign convinced the Jewish witnesses that Gentiles unquestionably had the right to be baptized. When Peter said, "Of a truth I perceive that God is no respecter of persons . . ." (Acts 10:34), he was saying, "At last, I understand." Peter realized that God and Christ were unconcerned about a person's origin or culture. God gladly accepted any person who reverenced Him and worked righteousness.

God's concept of beauty is distinctively different because it ignores cultural preferences and prejudices. Reverence and righteous living determine spiritual beauty. A righteous Oriental, Hispanic, Black, Indian, or Caucasian are of equal beauty to God.

*God never determines beauty by social rank or life circumstances.* Human opinions are strongly influenced by a person's living address, occupation, and social role. When a person speaks of having met some "beautiful people," rarely will those people be persons who are struggling to survive, persons who make their living by menial jobs, or persons who come from "backward" areas.

In contrast, God never notices those things when He considers beauty in people. Paul wrote,

> For ye are all sons of God, through faith, in Christ Jesus. For as many of you as were baptized into Christ did put on Christ. There can be neither Jew nor Greek, there can be neither bond nor free, there can be no male and female; for ye all are one man in Christ Jesus (Galatians 3:26–28).

All who have faith and are in Christ Jesus are God's children. All who have been baptized into Christ are in Christ. Regardless of social rank or life circumstances, everyone enters Christ precisely in the same manner — by baptism. The slave and the aristocrat, the rich and the poor, and all of every race enter Jesus in the same manner. Each by the same means becomes a child of God of equal value to God. There are no chosen people — no privileged Jews and inferior Gentiles; no privileged Americans and inferior foreigners; no slave and free citizen; no primitive third world people and sophisticated Americans; no privileged male and inferior female. God will as readily see beauty in a slave as in an aristocrat, in a woman as in a man.

## Beauty To God

What is beautiful in God's eyes? *Noting the qualities God has cherished in the lives of other people is one way to determine God's concept of beauty*. Noah's implicit trust in God led him to construct a mammoth boat miles from water. Abraham trusted God's promise so implicitly that he would have sacrificed his son of promise without hesitation. Moses yielded total control of his life to God and became the man of meekness. David committed his whole being to doing the will of God. No consequence or shameful treatment could keep Daniel from reverencing his God. People like Peter, Paul, Barnabas, and Timothy were ruled by God in every consideration and decision. They were totally preoccupied with Jesus' will as they shared the gospel with all. In all these qualities God saw great beauty.

While all these people were beautiful to God, virtually nothing is known about their physical appearance. It was not their physique or stateliness but their faith and service that made them beautiful to God. The same was true of God's beautiful women: Rahab, Hannah, Ruth, Deborah, and Mary Magdalene. Those noted for physical beauty were often great spiritual disappointments. Physically beautiful Sarah did not have the faith of Abraham. Saul was handsome, but he was not the godly king God wanted.

*The qualities God wants in His people further reveal His concept of beauty.* The beatitudes reveal some of God's standards of beauty. An awareness of one's spiritual poverty, sorrow for wickedness, hungering and thirsting after righteousness, being merciful, having purity of heart, and being a peacemaker are all qualities of beauty. The epistles also stress attributes valued by God: keeping a living faith while enduring physical hardships, controlling the tongue, enduring personal harm to protect the church's influence, making sacrifices for the good of others, and living by Christian convictions in the face of ridicule. All these are beautiful to God.

The beauty visible to God is the beauty of the inner person. No artificial spiritual cosmetics can improve one's appearance to God. Spiritual beauty does not arise from a pretended image. The person within the body who governs its actions is the source of beauty to God.

What is ugly to God? There is an ugly in God's sight. Do Judas, Ananias, and Sapphira produce a feeling of beauty or ugliness? Many in every age have been ugly in God's sight. Arrogance, deceit, sacrificing the innocent, scheming for wicked purposes, running to trouble, perjury, and creating division are ugly to God (Proverbs 6:16–19). Other ugly people include those who live for pleasure, the selfish, the faithless, those who indulge their passions, those who love money, and those who discourage the righteous. Those who are controlled by sin are ugly in God's sight.

## Spiritual Beauty Acquired

Every person has the power in Christ to change his spiritual appearance. No person has to be ugly in God's sight. Jesus can change any ugly "me" into a beautiful "me" by forgiveness and by teaching one how to live. The most beautiful Christians alive at one time were ugly sinners. No one inherits spiritual beauty; everyone develops such beauty by living in Christ.

*Every beautiful spiritual quality can be produced in a person who belongs to Christ and lets Christ rule his life.* Through His Word, Jesus can teach anyone how to live. Through faith Jesus can give anyone the power to live a new life.

*Every ugly spiritual quality can be destroyed by Christ.* Every past sin can be forgiven and erased from God's memory (Hebrews 8:12). One can learn how to endure temptations (I Corinthians 10:13). Provision has been made for the inevitable mistakes a Christian will make (I John 1:9–2:2).

A warning is in order. A beautiful appearance through neglect can become horribly ugly. A beautiful life of righteousness can become horribly ugly through neglect. Spiritual beauty must never be taken for granted nor be neglected. It must be remembered it is possible to be one of society's most impressive people and be one of the ugliest persons God knows. It is also possible to be an unknown in society and to be radiantly beautiful in the eyes of God. What God sees when He looks at a person is determined by the person alone.

## Questions

1. What are the distinguishing qualities that separate "beautiful" from "ugly"?
2. How do outward, physical appearances impress God? Where does God see beauty?
3. Why is it difficult for people of one culture to see beauty in people of another culture? Use the Jewish attitude toward Samaritans to illustrate the difficulty.
4. What does Acts 10:34 teach concerning God's attitude toward people of differing cultures?
5. How does a person's social rank and life circumstances influence others' thinking about him? Illustrate your answer.
6. Discuss Galatians 3:26–28 in regard to God's feelings and attitudes toward people.
7. Using qualities God has admired in people, make a list of qualities which are beautiful to God.
8. State and describe some beautiful qualities the New Testament declares God wants in people.
9. List some qualities which are "ugly" to God.
10. Explain this statement: every person has the power in Christ to change totally his spiritual appearance. How can this be done?

## *Thought Questions*

1. Why should Christians be concerned about being beautiful in God's eyes?
2. Why is it easy to believe that outward appearances are more important than inward being? What will this belief do to a Christian?
3. How can a person increase his beauty in God's eyes? Be practical and be specific.
4. Do people who are "ugly" to God know it? Explain your answer.
5. What is the most important lesson in this chapter?

# Chapter Thirteen

# Fires In My Bones

O Jehovah, thou has persuaded me, and I was persuaded; thou art stronger than I, and hast prevailed: I am become a laughing-stock all the day, everyone mocketh me. For as often as I speak, I cry out; I cry, Violence and destruction! because the word of Jehovah is made a reproach unto me, and a derision, all the day. And if I say, I will not make mention of him, nor speak any more in his name, then there is in my heart as it were a burning fire shut up in my bones, and I am weary with forbearing, and I cannot contain. For I have heard the defaming of many, terror on every side. Denounce, and we will denounce him, say all my familiar friends, they that watch for my fall; peradventure he will be persuaded, and we shall prevail against him and we shall take our revenge on him. But Jehovah is with me as a mighty one and a terrible: therefore my persecutors shall stumble, and they shall not prevail; they shall be utterly put to shame, because they have not dealt wisely, even with an everlasting dishonor which shall never be forgotten. But, O Jehovah of hosts, that triest the righteous, that seest the heart and the mind, let me see thy vengeance on them; for unto thee have I revealed my cause. Sing unto Jehovah, praise ye Jehovah; for he hath delivered the soul of the needy from the hand of evildoers (Jeremiah 20:7–13).

While the divine missions of many Bible people seem heroic and adventuresome, no one would want the missions of some of God's great servants. Jeremiah had one of those undesirable missions. He prophesied to Judea and Jerusalem for over forty years declaring the fall of Jerusalem and the Babylonian captivity. The early recipients of his prophecies were prosperous, secure, confident of the future, and wicked.

In Jeremiah's day it was fashionable to be wicked. The Jews went to the temple, called upon God, and declared their faith in His deliverance. They departed from worship to live as they pleased (Jeremiah 7:8–11). Because God's temple sat in Jerusalem, they were certain God would protect them (Jeremiah 7:1–7). Because they lived in *the* city of God, they regarded the suggestion that Jerusalem would fall as stupid and ridiculous.

Jeremiah's mission was to tell these people, "God will no longer overlook your sin. You are not God's people. A pagan enemy will destroy this city and take you into foreign captivity." It takes no imagination to realize Jeremiah's unpopularity as he declared his message (see Jeremiah 5).

To illustrate the unpopular nature of Jeremiah's mission, suppose God sent a special message to your preacher for the town. He is to declare publicly, "Because of your wickedness, God is going to utterly destroy this town. All will stand helpless before the enemy and lose everything he possesses." The congregation reacts to this public embarrassment by denying him the pulpit. No church will allow him in their building. The street is the only place he can proclaim his message. Day after day, year after year, he proclaims, "Because of the adultery, the deceitfulness, the sensuality, the drunkenness, and the hypocritical religious activities, God will destroy this town."

How would the public react to this man? He would be known as the "crazy old preacher." He would be laughed at, mocked, and abused. If a newcomer inquired, "Who is that?" he would be told, "That is the crazy old preacher who thinks God will destroy this town. Ignore him."

## Jeremiah's Predicament

This was Jeremiah's predicament as he fulfilled his mission. *He was hated and ignored, and few took him seriously.* Though his message was rejected, he knew it would happen. Thus his message became an enormous burden to him. The text reveals the intense, on-going inner struggle in his life.

*He was a continual laughingstock.* Being laughed at is painfully humiliating. The strong sense of rejection and degradation makes one wish to avoid the laughers. Though their laughter hurt Jeremiah, he returned and again declared the message to the laughers.

*He was mocked.* The pain of being mimicked and ridiculed quickly generates hot anger. Even to be mimicked jokingly hurts and humiliates. The hurt of mockery is biting and bitter. Though he despised the mockery, he declared the message.

*The message itself became his reproach.* The prophecy itself was a source of derision. The people did not want to hear what God told him to say. Even the few who believed him probably thought him foolish for his constant public declarations. No one thanked him for his message, appreciated his commitment, admired his faith, or respected him. No doubt everyone knew him and instantly recognized his message. That message doomed him to be "crazy old Jeremiah" who thought Jerusalem would fall.

Though Scripture does not record the insults hurled at him, they are easily imagined. "Jeremiah, was Jerusalem still standing when you got up today?" "Did you see the enemy coming today?" "Be careful when you leave the city, Jeremiah. The enemy is hiding in the hills." Each barb of ridicule likely produced a howl of laughter.

*Others tried to scare Jeremiah into silence.* The king, the counselors, and the aristocrats did not appreciate a "crazy man" scaring people about an imagined, impending invasion. Such ideas would irritate politicians and anger merchants. Who wants anyone continually hollering war and defeat? They did not silence Jeremiah, but they did terrify him.

*His friends would denounce him when he prophesied "that same stupid sermon" again.* They also watched for his fall. They yearned to see him fail as a prophet, and they tried to convince him he was wrong.

Can a more discouraging, disheartening task be imagined? While Jeremiah endured all this, he knew the prophecy was true. His persecutors and tormentors were wrong; they would fall. They would be utterly shamed and humiliated by an unforgettable, everlasting dishonor. Though he hoped to see God's vengeance, that hope was of no comfort. The first statement following the text is, "Cursed be the day wherein I was born."

## Why Continue?

Why did Jeremiah continue prophesying? Why not stop? He gives three reasons for continuing. First, God persuaded him. He knew God wanted the message proclaimed and wanted him to proclaim it. God's persuasiveness would not let him refuse. Second, God was stronger than he. He had struggled against his mission seriously considering rejecting the responsibility. However, his dissatisfaction was no match for the strength of God's determination. Third, there was a fire in his bones. There were moments when he closed his mouth and refused to speak. In those moments, the message's urgency and truthfulness refused to be denied. It was a fire burning in his bones.

The figure of fire in the bones is powerfully descriptive. A burn produces constant pain; nothing cools the fire in burned flesh. Imagine the continuing, deep pain of a fire in the marrow of the bones. Such pain would so obsess a person it could not be ignored. In the same manner Jeremiah's message obsessed him. In all his misery, Jeremiah prophesied because fire burned in his bones.

## A Beneficial Fire

Every Christian who wishes to walk with God on earth and to live with God in heaven should pray for fire in his bones. *First, he should pray that his desire for knowledge and understanding of God's Word become such a fire.* An undeniable sense of urgency must motivate him to be a constant student of the Word. His hunger for knowledge and understanding must be undeniable. He wants a clear, full understanding which enables him to share God's Word intelligently. When frustration and weariness discourage him, he wants to be powerless to quit learning and sharing.

*Second, he should pray that his concern for people, for their needs and for their salvation become a fire in his bones.* He wants the compassion, kindness, meekness, and forgiving spirit which lived in Jesus to burn within him. He never wishes to be content to teach or to counsel out of a sense of duty. He wishes to be ruled by the same sense of caring which ruled Jesus. When he is tired, when he has been hurt, when his caring has been spurned, or when he has been unjustly criticized, he wants the fire to keep the caring alive.

*Third, he should pray that his commitment to moral practices and ethical principles become a fire in his bones.* If society calls evil good and good evil, he never wants to confuse the two. If dishonesty becomes acceptable and profitable, he wants to honor truth, to keep his word, and to keep confidences in all circumstances. If Christians reject responsibility by rationalization and ignore right, he wants to heed all righteousness. He wants the fire to demand he walk uprightly even if he must walk alone.

*Fourth, he should pray that his acceptance of his responsibility to use himself for the good of the Lord become a fire in his bones.* He wants the heat of that fire to evaporate selfishness as he remembers he does not belong to himself. The memory of Jesus the Servant is to fuel the fire. When tempted to think that he serves too much, works too hard, or is unjustly burdened, he wants to see his folly immediately. He wants the fire to make it impossible to salve his conscience with rationalizations or excuses.

The prayer for such a fire is the desire to be filled with an undeniable sense of need and urgency. It is the desire to be unable to neglect God's purposes or restrain godly forces within himself. It is the yearning to be as helpless before God's purposes as was Jeremiah.

Unfortunately, some Christians regard the desire for such fire as ridiculous. "Why pray to be possessed in that manner? Such commitment would create many crises and problems. Why not seek a spiritual life of convenience?" A New Testament Christian *NEVER* wants merely to call himself a Christian. *THE* priority of life is to succeed spiritually in Christ. Regardless of the cost, he wants to do God's will. The successful Christian's greatest asset is fire in the bones. He cherishes the fire because he cherishes spiritual success.

## Questions

1. Jeremiah is called the "crying prophet." Using Jeremiah 11:18–23, 15:10–21, 17:12–18, and 18:18–23, explain why that designation is appropriate.
2. Why were the inhabitants of Jerusalem difficult to warn?
3. List the ways in which people sought to discourage Jeremiah. Discuss the hurt each would produce.
4. Explain how Jeremiah's message became a reproach to him.
5. Why would Jeremiah's message have irritated public officials and prominent people?
6. Was Jeremiah seriously discouraged? Explain your answer.
7. What were the three reasons which caused Jeremiah to continue?
8. Explain what Jeremiah meant by having "fire in his bones."

9. Explain why a Christian should pray for a fire in his bones in
   the following matters:
   a. The desire for knowledge and understanding of God's
      Word.
   b. Concern for people, their needs, and their salvation.
   c. Commitment to moral and ethical living.
   d. Acceptance of the responsibility to use self for the Lord's
      good.
10. When one prays for fires in his bones, for what is he praying?
    Why does he want such fire?

## Thought Questions

1. What do you regard as the strongest discouragement Jeremiah
   faced?
2. What are some of the strong personal discouragements Christians face today?
3. Explain why it is valuable for a Christian to be powerless to
   quit doing God's will. What is meant by "powerless" to quit?
4. Why is it difficult to pray seriously and honestly for fire in the
   bones?
5. What is the most important lesson you have learned in this
   chapter?

## Review Thought Question

What are the most helpful lessons about Christian living which
you have learned from this study?

I

♡

John